discard

THE LINCOLN MURDER PLOT

THE LINCOLN

MURDER PLOT

BY KAREN ZEINERT

LINNET BOOKS   1999

First published 1999 as a Linnet Book,
an imprint of The Shoe String Press, Inc.,
North Haven, Connecticut 06473.

Library of Congress Cataloging-in-Publication Data

Zeinert, Karen.
    The Lincoln murder plot / by Karen Zeinert.
        p. cm.
    Includes bibliographical references and index.
    Summary: Text, including quotations from contemporary sources such
as the diary of John Wilkes Booth, the testimony of witnesses, letters, and
accounts by others involved, examines the assassination of President
Abraham Lincoln.
    ISBN 0-208-02451-4 (lib. bdg. : alk. paper).
   1. Lincoln, Abraham, 1809–1865—Assassination—Juvenile literature.
[1. Lincoln, Abraham, 1809–1865—Assassination.] I. Title.
E457.5.Z45   1999
973.7'092—dc21   98-36971
                                     CIP
                                        AC

Designed by Abigail Johnston
Printed in the United States of America

TO ARLO SELL AND JEAN BATTERMAN,

WHO LOVE BOOKS AS MUCH AS I DO

CONTENTS

INTRODUCTION

On April 14, 1865, John Wilkes Booth shot President Abraham Lincoln, who died the following day. It was the first assassination of an American president, and the murder horrified and sickened the public. Although many Americans demanded immediate revenge for this shocking crime, the rapid roundup of suspects, their trials, and their punishments—especially the executions—eventually enraged most citizens. They wondered aloud about the proceedings. Had the witnesses told the truth in the courtroom? Had all of the evidence been made public? Were others besides the accused involved in the Lincoln murder plot? If so, who were they? The following pages examine the controversy that surrounded the president's death. The information will help you determine the answer to the most important question of all: Was justice served in the aftermath of the assassination?

CAST OF CHARACTERS

The Lincoln assassination plot involves many people, some of whom are important in the beginning of the story and do not reappear until the end. This list, which contains the main characters, famous, infamous, and unknown, will help you refresh your memory.

Arnold, Samuel—one of Booth's co-conspirators
Atzerodt, George—one of Booth's co-conspirators
Bingham, John—a prosecutor in the assassination trial
Booth, John Wilkes—shot Abraham Lincoln
Burnett, Henry—a prosecutor in the assassination trial
Clay, Clement—advisor to Jefferson Davis
Conover, Sanford—his testimony supposedly linked the South
    to the Lincoln assassination plot
Davis, David—Supreme Court justice
Davis, Jefferson—president of the Confederacy

Grant, Ulysses S.—Union general

Herold, David—Booth's co-conspirator, captured with Booth

Holt, Joseph—judge advocate in assassination trial, main prosecutor

Johnson, Andrew—Lincoln's second vice president

Lincoln, Abraham—sixteenth president of the United States; first to be assassinated

Lloyd, John—rented Mary Surratt's tavern, testified at assassination trial

Mudd, Samuel—doctor who treated Booth

O'Laughlin, Michael—Booth's co-conspirator

Paine, Lewis—Booth's co-conspirator

Parker, John—guard outside presidential box in Ford's Theatre on the night of Lincoln's assassination

Seward, William—Lincoln's secretary of state, severely wounded during assassination attempt

Spangler, Edward—stagehand accused of helping Booth escape

Stanton, Edwin—Secretary of War, headed investigation of Lincoln's assassination

Surratt, Mary—one of the defendants in the assassination trial

Surratt, John—one of Booth's co-conspirators, Mary's son

Weichmann, Louis—witness at assassination trial

TIMELINE

1860

November 6—Abraham Lincoln is elected president of the United States.

December 20—South Carolina secedes (leaves the Union). Other slave states begin to vote on secession. Eventually eleven Southern states (Alabama, Arkansas, Florida, Georgia, Louisiana, Mississippi, North Carolina, South Carolina, Tennessee, Texas, and Virginia) form the Confederate States of America. Representatives elect Jefferson Davis president.

1861

April 12—The first shots of the Civil War are fired at Fort Sumter, near Charleston, South Carolina.

April 15—President Lincoln prepares to use massive force against the Confederacy to reunite the country.

1863

Early July—Vicksburg, Mississippi, falls to Union troops. At the same time, Confederate forces in the East are defeated at Gettysburg, Pennsylvania. These battles are turning points in the war. The Confederacy is now seriously weakened.

1864

Spring—The North decides to stop exchanging prisoners of war with the South in an attempt to severely limit the number of soldiers available to the South.

November 8—Lincoln is reelected. His running mate is Andrew Johnson, a Democrat. They represent the Union Party, a coalition of Republicans and Democrats.

1865

March 4—Lincoln is inaugurated for his second term.

April 2—The Confederates are forced to abandon Richmond.

April 9—General Robert E. Lee surrenders his troops to General U.S. Grant at Appomattox Court House, Virginia.

April 10—Huge celebrations marking the end of the war begin in the North.

April 14—Lincoln is shot by John Wilkes Booth, and Secretary of State William Seward is attacked by Lewis Paine.

April 15—Lincoln dies. Detectives look for John Surratt, a friend of Booth's. Booth and David Herold, an accomplice, seek medical help from Dr. Samuel Mudd. They leave Mudd's home later that day and spend six days hiding in the wilderness.

April 17—Samuel Arnold, Michael O'Laughlin, Mary

Surratt, and Lewis Paine are arrested. Mudd is questioned for the first time.

April 19—The first funeral for Lincoln is held in Washington, D.C. Edward Spangler is arrested.

April 21—Lincoln's funeral train leaves Washington, D.C.

April 24—Mudd is arrested.

April 26—Herold is captured and Booth is shot to death on Garrett's farm in northern Virginia.

May 2—President Johnson announces that Confederate officials were behind Lincoln's assassination. Johnson offers rewards for the arrest for six Southerners, including Jefferson Davis.

May 4—Lincoln's body arrives in Springfield for the last of his twelve official funerals.

May 6—President Johnson appoints a military commission to try eight people suspected of being part of the Lincoln murder plot.

May 9—The conspirators' trial begins.

May 10—Jefferson Davis is captured.

May 26—The last of the Confederate troops surrender.

June 30—The military commission finalizes its verdicts and recommendations for punishment.

July 6—The commission's decisions are announced.

July 7—Paine, Herold, Atzerodt, and Mary Surratt are hanged.

July 17—Mudd, Arnold, Spangler, and O'Laughlin are imprisoned on Dry Tortugas.

1866

April 9—The House of Representatives tells its Judiciary

Committee to begin an investigation of the Jefferson Davis case.

July—Sanford Conover's testimony is exposed as a lie.

Late 1866—The Supreme Court announces its decision in the Milligan case.

November 27—John Surratt is arrested.

1867

May 13—Jefferson Davis is released from prison.

June 10—John Surratt's trial begins.

August 12—President Johnson fires Edwin Stanton.

1868

February 21—The House of Representatives begins its impeachment of President Johnson.

May 26—The Senate finds Johnson not guilty.

1869

February 8—Johnson pardons Mudd, Arnold, and Spangler.

March—Johnson orders the exhumation of the bodies of Booth, Surratt, Paine, Herold, and Atzerodt so that they can be returned to their families.

1876

Summer—Jim Kneally makes plans to steal Lincoln's body.

1901

September 26—Lincoln is buried for the last time.

1937

Otto Eisenschiml's book *Why Was Lincoln Murdered?* is published.

1961

Ray Neff claims to have found a letter written by Lafayette Baker, one of the men who buried Booth.

1977

David Balsiger and Charles Sellier, Jr., publish *The Lincoln Conspiracy*, which is supposedly based on the missing pages from Booth's diary.

1 A GRAND CONSPIRACY

Clergymen began to ring church bells in Washington, D.C., shortly before dawn on Monday, April 10, 1865. The loud, joyous clanging woke the townspeople, and they poured into the city's streets—many still in their sleepwear—to hear the eagerly anticipated news. The rumors, messengers said, were true. General Robert E. Lee had surrendered on Sunday to General Ulysses S. Grant at Appomattox Court House. Even though some troops remained in the field, the Civil War was over.

Washingtonians had waited a long time for this moment, and the good news was greeted with an outburst of emotion, a mix of overwhelming relief and unlimited joy. Men, women, and children cried, fell to their knees to give prayers of thanksgiving, cheered, chanted, and danced in the streets. Saloon owners threw open their doors and more than a few people entered, making toast after toast to the Union, President Abraham Lincoln, and General Grant. As the day wore on, townspeople paraded throughout the city, waving flags, tooting horns, and singing and shouting until they were hoarse. A few citizens even dressed up in silly costumes. It was Christmas, New Year's Eve, and the Fourth of July all rolled into one celebration. And it was quite a sight.

The hoopla in the capital—as well as throughout the rest of the North—continued for four more days. Schools and businesses were closed for at least part of this time, making it possible for children and workers to join jubilant throngs in the streets. To add to the festivities, homeowners and officials decorated the city. They draped houses and public buildings with red, white, and blue bunting and raised the Stars and Stripes on every flagpole in the city. In the evening, people placed candles and lanterns in as many windows as possible, and at a designated time, they lit the wicks, creating what was then known as a "grand illumination," a display reserved for very special occasions.

Few people minded the large crowds, deafening noise, or growing confusion that the celebrations caused. Most citizens were simply too happy to complain about anything. More than one million soldiers could come home now, and death and dying, so the people thought, would no longer dominate the headlines. President Lincoln spoke for many when he said, "I've never been so happy in my life."[1]

Washington had not seen such jubilation since the war began in 1861, when many Americans were eager for battle. Both the North and the South had believed that they were right, and they were more than willing to use force to prove their points. Both sides also believed that the conflict would be short and glorious. But the North underestimated the South's determination to leave the Union, and Southerners misjudged the North's will to hold the country together. The short war everyone had anticipated—sixty days long at the most—became a four-year ordeal of hard-fought, bloody battles.

By 1865, more than 600,000 men had died in the conflict. This tragic loss is nearly equal to the number of American casualties in all of America's other wars combined—the Revolutionary War (1775-1783), the War of 1812 (1812-1815), the Mexican War (1846-1848), the Spanish-American War (1898), World War I (1917-1918), World War II (1941-1945), the Korean Conflict (1950-1953), the war in Vietnam (1965-1975), and the Persian Gulf War (1991). In short, the losses were staggering, and it is no wonder that Americans were overjoyed when they heard that the bloodshed had finally come to an end.

Understandably, the mood in the South was anything but jubilant after Lee surrendered. Here sorrow, despair, and bitterness, not joy, had been the dominant emotions for some time. Many, like Nellie Grey, who lived in Richmond, the Confederate capital, had begun their mourning for the death of the Confederacy as soon as federal troops entered the capital on April 3. Most Southerners believed, correctly, that the city's fall signaled the end of the war. Grey said, "We covered our faces and cried. . . . All through the house was the sound of sobbing. It was as the house of mourning, the house of death."[2]

During the celebrations in Washington, people wanted to get a glimpse of President Lincoln and General Grant, so their whereabouts were routinely reported in the papers. When an announcement was made that both Lincoln and Grant would be

ABRAHAM LINCOLN

Although Abraham Lincoln is now one of the best known and most beloved of all American presidents, he was not popular when elected to the presidency in 1860. Southerners believed that Lincoln was an abolitionist, and as a result, he failed to get a *single* vote in eleven slave states. On the other hand, many Northerners, who hoped that Lincoln was an abolitionist, thought that he was uneducated, inexperienced, and downright vulgar, and when they voted for him, they did so with great reservation.

Even though Lincoln's background was certainly humble, he was not the ruffian that critics made him out to be. It was true that Lincoln, who was born in a log cabin in Kentucky in 1809, had less than one year of formal schooling. However, he had studied on his own, achieving a remarkable education and earning a license to practice law in the process. And he was no newcomer to politics. After settling in Illinois as a young man, he had successfully run for the Illinois legislature in 1834, where he served until 1841. Six years later, after abandoning a thriving legal practice in Springfield, he had successfully run for Congress, serving one term as a representative in Washington, D.C.

Much has been written about his marriage to Mary Todd Lincoln, whom he met in Springfield and married in 1842. Although Mary had a bad temper and suffered from depression at times, most historians believe that they were a devoted couple. They had four sons: Eddie, who died in Springfield; Willie, who died while Lincoln was president; Tad; and Robert.

As the war dragged on with no end in sight, frustrated Northerners, afraid to attack Lincoln, lashed out at Mary. Critics questioned her taste in clothing, her spending habits, and, because her brothers were fighting for the South, her loyalty. The attacks took their toll, and, when Lincoln was assassinated, Mary's mental state was shaky at best. When Tad died a few years later, she had an emotional breakdown and was committed to a mental institution for a while. She died in 1882. *Photo courtesy of the Library of Congress.*

attending a performance in Ford's Theatre on the night of April 14, Good Friday, people rushed to buy tickets for the same show.

That night, the president's carriage slowly threaded its way through crowds of people in the streets. Lincoln and his wife were cheered as they passed by. A few spectators were disappointed, however, when they realized that General Grant and his wife were not in the carriage. The Grants' daughter had just arrived in Washington, and she was insistent upon seeing her parents at once. Her arrival gave the Grants a good reason to turn down the Lincolns' invitation. Besides, Grant wasn't especially fond of plays, and Mrs. Grant did not like Mrs. Lincoln. When the Grants declined, Major Henry Reed Rathbone and his stepsister and fiancée, Clara Harris, accompanied the Lincolns.

About 8:30, half an hour after the play *Our American Cousin* began, the president and his party arrived. As usual, they were shown to boxes seven and eight, which had been specially prepared. The partition between the two boxes had been removed so that the foursome could be as comfortable as possible, and a sofa for the major, chairs for the women, and a rocking chair for the president had been carefully arranged for the best views. For decoration, huge flags were draped beneath the boxes, which overlooked the stage.

When actress Laura Keene saw Lincoln arrive, she stopped her presentation. The band then struck up "Hail to the Chief," and everyone in the theatre rose, turned toward the president, and applauded loudly.

Although Lincoln had received many threats on his life during the war, especially after his reelection in 1864, he usually resisted protection. After all, he repeatedly pointed out, no American president had ever been assassinated. Now that the war was over, he argued, there was little to be gained by killing him. So tonight, although the soldiers who had escorted him to the theatre stood guard outside, only one policeman, John Parker, was on duty inside the building.

About 9:30, John Wilkes Booth, a famous actor, entered the theatre. Because he had often performed here, no one was surprised to see him. As a result, he moved about without causing suspicion, although his clothing—riding attire complete with leather boots and silver spurs—did raise a few eyebrows. So did the fact that he had left a horse just outside the back door. Booth had asked Edward Spangler, a stagehand and good friend, to hold his horse's reins, insisting that the high-spirited mare would escape if tied to a hitching post. Spangler was too busy to do this, so he recruited a boy known as Peanuts John to take care of the mount.

Once inside the theatre, Booth strolled throughout the building, examining it carefully for any last-minute changes. He also listened carefully to the dialogue to determine how far the play, which he knew well, had progressed. After checking his watch, he left for a nearby tavern, where he rapidly downed several drinks.

Booth reentered the theatre about 10:00 P.M., and he went directly to the door of the small, dark hall that led to the presidential boxes. This door was not guarded—for some unknown reason, Parker had left his post—and Booth was able to enter the hall with ease. Once inside, he placed a brace against the door to

JOHN WILKES BOOTH

John Wilkes Booth was born on the family farm near Bel Air, Maryland, in 1838. The farm consisted of a mansion called Tudor Hall, stables, barns, slave quarters, and a large pond. The family also owned a town house in nearby Baltimore. John was one of six children. His parents were Ann and Junius Booth, who was a famous Shakespearean actor. John was named for one of his father's heroes, John Wilkes, an English political reformer who supported the American colonists during the Revolutionary War. John Wilkes Booth was so taken by stories about Wilkes that he sometimes dropped his last name, calling himself simply John Wilkes.

Like his father and two of his brothers, John chose to become an actor. By 1860 he was a star, playing before packed theatres in the South. He earned more than $20,000 a year at a time when the average worker's annual income was less than $1,000. As his fame spread, so did the demand for his performances. Between 1861 and 1864, Booth appeared on stage throughout the North and South, as well as in parts of Canada. It was during this time that he smuggled medications—and probably information—into the South in one of his many trunks filled with costumes.

John Wilkes Booth was the only member of his family to argue for the Southern cause. Always looking for supporters, he tried to convert his broth-

ers, turning many a family gathering into a disaster. He defended slavery and insisted that the South had a right to fight for its freedom, just as the colonists did so many years before. The more desperate the situation became for the South, the more devoted Booth became to its cause. *Photo courtesy of the Library of Congress.*

prevent anyone from opening it. He then proceeded to a small hole that he had made earlier in the day in the door of the president's boxes. Booth shut an eye, peered through the opening, and studied Lincoln, who was outlined by light from the stage.

At the same time, Booth concentrated on the play's dialogue. When only one actor, Harry Hawk, was on stage and he was about to deliver a line sure to cause loud laughter, Booth opened the door. No one noticed him. No light entered the box because the outer room was dark, and everyone's attention was riveted on the stage. Booth aimed his single-shot derringer and waited for the audience's expected reaction. When the people hooted and howled, Booth fired. The bullet entered the president's head behind his left ear as planned.

It took but a second for those in the presidential party to realize that something dreadful had happened. Mrs. Lincoln saw her husband's head fall to his chest, and as his body began to slump in his chair, she screamed. At the same time, Major Rathbone smelled the smoke from the firearm. He turned around to find the source, spotted the intruder, and rose to grab hold of him. Booth responded by drawing his knife and slashing the major, cutting his arm to the bone.

When Rathbone reeled back in pain and shock, Booth charged to the front of the box and jumped to the stage below. But as he did so, he caught his right spur in one of the flags draped beneath the box. This caused him to land off-balance, and, as he hit the stage, he fractured a bone in his left leg. Ignoring his pain and always the actor, he turned toward the audience and shouted. Not everyone agreed upon what was said,

While attending a play at Ford's Theatre on April 14, 1865, President Lincoln was assassinated by John Wilkes Booth. Today the restored theatre hosts special presentations and serves as a memorial to Lincoln, who loved the performing arts. *Photo by Carol Highsmith, courtesy of the Parks & History Association.*

The presidential box in Ford's Theatre from which Lincoln and his party watched the play *Our American Cousin.* After shooting Lincoln, John Wilkes Booth jumped from the box, catching a spur on the bunting and landing with a broken leg on the stage below. *Photo by Bill Clark, courtesy of the National Park Service.*

although most thought that his words were "*Sic semper tyrannis,*" Latin for "Thus always to tyrants."

At first, members of the audience were confused. Was this part of the play? they wondered. After all, the man on the stage, whom many recognized, was an actor.

The cast and crew, however, were not confused. Harry Hawk knew that Booth wasn't part of *Our American Cousin,* nor was his bloody knife a prop. Furthermore, Major Rathbone and Clara Harris were both shouting, begging someone—anyone!—to stop the assailant. But when Hawk started toward Booth, Booth raised his knife in the air, readying himself to attack. This forced Hawk to retreat. William Withers, the orchestra leader, then started toward Booth. When Withers was within striking distance, Booth repeatedly swung the tip of his knife at the musician, shredding his jacket and frightening him away as well. The path to the back door was now clear.

While Booth made his exit, the audience looked toward the boxes where the actor had been, to try to make sense of the strange scene before them. They heard Clara Harris plead for a doctor, and they saw Mrs. Lincoln, who was crying, try to hold her husband upright. Clearly, this was not part of a make-believe comedy; it was nothing less than a real-life tragedy.

Mayhem followed in the packed theatre. One of the men in the audience, Joseph B. Stewart, and at least one stagehand charged after Booth. While they raced toward the exit, most members of the audience tried to reach the entrance to escape from the horror they had just witnessed. They were hindered by a group of people trying to get to the president. When some men and women finally managed to reach the street and told crowds there what had happened, many of these people pushed their way into the theatre, as did the soldiers who had stood guard outside. The result was a lot of shoving, shouting, crying and cursing—and an abrupt end to the celebrations.

Although his wounded arm was nearly numb, Major Rathbone was somehow able to remove the brace that Booth had placed against the door. This made it possible for two doctors, Charles Augustus Leale and Charles Sabin Taft, to enter the presidential boxes. After examining Lincoln's wound, both agreed that it was fatal.

Since Lincoln could not endure even a short journey to the White House, the doctors decided to try to find a room for him near the theatre. Lacking a stretcher, Lincoln was carried on a shutter through a growing mass of people who were so intent upon seeing him that soldiers had to draw their swords to part the crowd. The president was finally taken to the Petersen boarding-house across the street. Shortly after, the death watch began, as family, friends, and government officials rushed to Lincoln's side.

As if this tragedy wasn't enough, word reached the crowds waiting in the streets that someone had tried to assassinate the secretary of state, William H. Seward, at the very moment that Booth had shot Lincoln. The unidentified assailant had entered Seward's home on the pretext of delivering medicine to the secretary, who was recovering from a carriage accident. Once inside, the man had wreaked havoc on the Seward household. After attacking Seward's son, who stood before his father's bedroom door, beating the son with a pistol until the gun broke, the assailant had entered the secretary's bedroom and attempted to kill Seward. Two family members and a male nurse had defended the secretary, putting up such a valiant fight that the assailant had been forced to flee. As he headed for the door, he had encountered and stabbed a State Department messenger.

The two shocking events convinced Washingtonians that a grand conspiracy was afoot, a last-minute, desperate attempt on the part of the Confederates to win the war. Who else would do such a thing? people asked. Hadn't Southerners been threatening to kill Lincoln for some time now? Didn't someone actually place an ad in a Southern newspaper offering to kill Lincoln and his whole cabinet if Southerners would pay $1 million for the job?[3] This had to be the work of the South. Hang the rebels! the crowds shouted. And hang them high!

Anger, despair, and fear, plus the fact that the incredible had actually happened, created the perfect atmosphere for rumormongers. As a result, stories that would never have been believed otherwise were accepted without question. The entire cabinet was dead, some said, as well as all the generals. Others reported that the treaty at Appomattox was a hoax. The war was still on, and Confederate soldiers were heading toward a defenseless, leaderless Washington at that very moment.

Although government officials knew full well that the entire government had not been destroyed, officials, like the people, assumed that the attacks were the result of a grand conspiracy and that precautions had to be taken. So troops were dispatched to protect the vice president, the rest of the cabinet, and all Supreme Court justices. Generals were warned that assassins were loose and ready to kill. Secretary of War Edwin M. Stanton had already ordered soldiers manning exits on the outskirts of the city—a wartime curfew was still in effect—to catch Booth should he decide to flee the capital. Now Stanton instructed the men to watch for more than one killer. The sound of the call to arms and the sight of soldiers dashing here and there frightened the people even more. It was a very long night.

At 7:30 A.M. on April 15, for the second time in less than a week, clergymen rang every church bell in Washington. This time the pace was slow and steady. No one poured into the streets to hear the latest news; the streets were already full of anxious people. And there was no need for messengers to tell the crowds what the tolling meant. Everyone knew that the bells were announcing President Abraham Lincoln's death.

Sad, somber people stood in shock, and silence replaced the cheers of the last five days and the shouts about conspiracy from the night before. Instead of returning home, many awaited Lincoln's cortege, a group of mourners carrying the president's body back to the White House. This procession, according to Noah Brooks, in the street that day, created a heart-wrenching scene. As he and his friends wandered up F Street toward Ford's Theatre, he said:

> We met [the] tragical procession. It was headed by a
> group of army officers walking bareheaded, and behind
> them, carried tenderly by a company of soldiers, was

the bier of the dead President, covered with the flag of
the Union, and accompanied by an escort of soldiers
who had been on duty at the house where Lincoln
died. As the little cortege passed down the street to the
White House, every head was uncovered, and the pro-
found silence which prevailed was broken only by sobs
and by the sound of the [steps] of those who bore the
martyred President back to the house which he had so
lately quitted full of life, hope, and courage.[4]

Northerners immediately began an official period of mourning. Grief-stricken civil servants and citizens alike lowered their
flags and took down red, white, and blue decorations. Black became the color of the day—black armbands, black clothes, black
wreaths on doors, black bunting beneath windows, and a black
mood in the people's hearts.

Meanwhile, Lincoln's cabinet planned the president's funerals, twelve in all. After the first service in Washington on April
19, Lincoln's body was to be placed in a special train, nine cars
long, and taken to Baltimore, Maryland; Harrisburg and
Philadelphia, Pennsylvania; New York City, Albany, and
Buffalo, New York; Cleveland and Columbus, Ohio;
Indianapolis, Indiana; and Chicago and Springfield, Illinois,
Lincoln's home, where it was to arrive on May 4. A short, im-
promptu service was also held in Michigan City, Indiana,
where the train was stopped by hundreds of people who
wanted to honor Lincoln.

The mourning decorations on the Lincoln home in Springfield, Illinois, were typical of the day. Traditionally, black curtains flanked each window, and black squares of fabric outlined in white hung over each windowsill. White decorated the edge of the roof and columns of evergreen branches, signifying eternal life, were fastened to the four corners of the house. The people here are the official delegates sent from Chicago to attend Lincoln's last funeral. They are waiting for his body to arrive and the procession to the cemetery to begin. *Photo courtesy of the Illinois State Historical Library.*

The train left Washington on April 21, and at each stop along the way, the procedure was the same. The president's coffin was removed from the train, placed in a hearse, and driven through the city where citizens lined the streets to see it. The casket was then taken to a prearranged spot and opened so that people might view the body before a service was held. As many as eighty viewers per minute passed the coffin in New York City, about half a million people in all. In other cities, where only a few hours had been scheduled, as few as ten thousand saw Lincoln's body.

Three hundred mourners traveled in the train with the coffin. These included several family members, two cousins of Mary Todd Lincoln and two of her brothers-in-law. Mrs. Lincoln, who was too emotionally overwrought to attend any services, remained in Washington for several months with her children. Her son Robert attended the last funeral in Springfield. Senators and representatives, judges, soldiers, doctors, and an embalmer rode with the family representatives. The embalmer was one of the most important travelers, for it was he who readjusted Lincoln's body in the casket after each ride, straightening his clothes and combing his hair. He also dusted Lincoln's face with colored chalk to try to cover the discoloration that was becoming more obvious at each viewing.

A second coffin, that of Willie Lincoln, the president's son who died in the White House, also rode in the train. This coffin had been removed from a cemetery in the capital so that father and son could be buried side by side.

An estimated seven million Americans saw the president's funeral train or viewed his body. Twenty-five million attended unofficial funerals in their own churches on April 19. Instead of calming the people, the funerals seemed to fuel their emotions. Wherever Lincoln's body was put on display, soldiers guarding the casket often found it difficult to keep order as mourners pushed to see the body or tried to touch or kiss it.

Meanwhile, Southerners looked on with horror as Northerners mourned, raged, and shook their fists at the South. Southerners knew that Lincoln would have made reconciliation as easy as possible, and more than one believed that the South had lost the best friend that it had in the federal government. The future suddenly seemed more frightening than ever.

2 FIRST ARRESTS

Because the War Department was responsible for protecting government officials and arresting anyone who attacked or threatened them, it led the manhunt for John Wilkes Booth and each and every fellow conspirator. The most prominent men in the search were Edwin Stanton, the secretary of war, and Colonel Lafayette C. Baker, head of the War Department's detective force. Local policemen helped the department, often rounding up suspects for questioning.

The search for the assassin began in his room in the National Hotel in Washington. Booth was long gone, but he had left behind a Confederate cipher used to decode messages and a letter that pointed to two accomplices. This letter was written less than three weeks before Lincoln's assassination by a friend of Booth's identified only as "Sam."

Edwin Stanton was Lincoln's secretary of war from 1862 to 1865. Stanton organized the manhunt to bring in Lincoln's assassin and any and all who were associated with him. *Photo courtesy of the Library of Congress.*

[Baltimore County, Maryland]
March 27, 1865

Dear John:
Was business so important that you could not remain in Balto. till I saw you? I came in as soon as I could, but found you had gone to W - - - n. I called also to see Mike. . . . You know full well that the G - - -t suspects something is going on there; therefore the undertaking is becoming more complicated. Why not, for the present, desist? . . . Do not act rashly or in haste. I would prefer your first query, "Go and see how it will be taken at R - - - d."

Write me [in] Balto., as I expect to be in about Wednesday or Thursday, or, if you can possibly come on, I will Tuesday meet you in Balto., at B - - -. Ever I subscribe myself.

Your friend,
Sam[5]

As soon as Booth was identified as the assassin, James L. McPhail, provost marshal general of Baltimore, told War Department officials about two close friends of Booth's, Samuel Arnold and Michael O'Laughlin, whom McPhail had known since childhood. Both men, McPhail said, were staunch Confederate supporters, former soldiers, and long-time acquaintances of Booth's. They had attended school with the actor, although at different times, and O'Laughlin had been Booth's neighbor in Baltimore.

As a result of McPhail's information, Sam's letter took on great significance. Since the names "Sam" and "Mike" appeared in the document, it was proof positive, officials said, that Sam Arnold and Mike O'Laughlin were involved in the conspiracy. The Confederate cipher and the mention of Richmond (R - - - d) in the letter, although the meaning wasn't too clear, was thought to be proof of Southern involvement. On April 17, McPhail arrested twenty-eight-year-old Arnold at Fort Monroe in Virginia, where he had just started a new job. McPhail also took O'Laughlin into custody in

Samuel Bland Arnold and John
Wilkes Booth attended St. Timothy's
Hall, a prep school in Cantonsville,
Maryland, when they were
teenagers. Although Arnold's home
state of Maryland did not secede
from the Union, he believed so
strongly in the South's cause that he
enlisted in the Confederate Army.
When his term was up, he moved to
Baltimore. Arnold was one of the
first men to be recruited by Booth
for his kidnapping plot even though
he hadn't seen his old friend in
nearly thirteen years. *Photo courtesy of
the Library of Congress.*

Michael O'Laughlin was a child-
hood friend of John Wilkes Booth.
They were the same age, attended
elementary school together, and
played together as children. The
O'Laughlin family lived next door
to the Booth family's town house in
Baltimore. When the war began,
O'Laughlin, like fellow-conspirator
Arnold, joined the Confederate
Army. When he returned to
Baltimore, he was contacted by
Booth. *Photo courtesy of the Library of
Congress.*

Baltimore the same day. Both vehemently denied being part of the assassination plot.

Once these men were publicly identified, witnesses came forth with damning testimony against Michael O'Laughlin. On April 13, he had been seen at a grand illumination in Washington, where he had spent considerable time in front of the secretary of war's home. When General Grant, who was visiting the secretary, had ventured outside to greet well-wishers, O'Laughlin had insisted upon seeing him. A sergeant accompanying Grant had become alarmed by O'Laughlin's demands, and the officer had ordered him to leave the premises. Other witnesses had seen him visiting with Booth at his hotel that night shortly before the illumination. War Department officials concluded that Booth's friend was supposed to kill the general, and that on the night before Lincoln's assassination, he was scouting his prey.

Only hours after Lincoln was shot, several Washingtonians told War Department officials about Booth's friendship with John Surratt. At 2:00 A.M. on April 15, department officials sent local policemen to the Surratt boardinghouse at 541 H Street to question him. Louis Weichmann, one of the boarders, answered the door. When he informed the officers that John Surratt was not at home, the men insisted upon searching the house. Unable to grant such permission, Weichmann woke Mary Surratt, John's mother and owner of the house. She told the detectives that they could search the house, which they did. Failing to find any trace of John, they left.

Late at night on April 17, War Department detectives, armed

with new information, visited the boardinghouse. In early March, boarder Weichmann, a federal employee, had told his superior about suspicious events in the Surratt house—hushed conversations, strangers coming and going at all hours, and a stash of weapons in John's room. Because Weichmann had no proof of wrongdoing, his information, which now took on some importance, had not been passed on to the War Department.

In addition, detectives had received information about ties between the Surratt family and the Confederacy. A tavern about ten miles south of Washington, which Mrs. Surratt inherited from her husband and was now rented out to John Lloyd, had been a meeting place for Confederate spies throughout the war. Also, there were rumors that the boardinghouse in Washington had been a safe house for Southern couriers.

By this time, detectives probably knew that twenty-year-old John Surratt was one of these couriers. Since 1863, he had routinely carried messages from Richmond to Washington or Montreal, Canada, where a number of Confederate officials worked for the cause. These men, led by Southerners Jacob Thompson and Clement Clay, raised funds and tried to get England and her colony, Canada, to support the South. They also helped Southern prisoners of war, who managed to reach Canada after escaping from Northern prisons, to rejoin their army units again. In addition, the "Canadian cabinet" supported the Copperheads, Southern sympathizers in the North. Copperheads raised money for the South and worked hard to defeat President Lincoln when he ran for reelection in 1864.

MARY JENKINS SURRATT

Mary Eugenia Jenkins married John Surratt in 1835, and a few years later, they purchased a farm in northern Maryland. They opened a small tavern on part of the property. When this tavern began to serve as a local post office, John became the postmaster. From then on the site was known as Surrattsville. The Surratts had three children: Issac, who joined the Confederate Army when the South seceded; Anna; and John, Jr., who spied for the South.

At the beginning of the war, the Surratts had many slaves, a prosperous farm, a thriving tavern, and property in Washington, D.C. A few months later, Union troops destroyed their crops as the soldiers marched toward Virginia, and their slaves ran off in search of a better life. When John, Sr. died in 1862, Mary, unable to run the tavern by herself and needing an income, decided to rent the tavern to John Lloyd and move to her property in Washington.

Several of the conspirators lived in her Washington home, which she converted into a boardinghouse, and Booth often visited them. Her connections to the conspirators and the fact that she knew Booth made her a prime suspect in the Lincoln plot investigation. *Photo courtesy of the National Archives.*

Because of the latest information, all of the Surratts were now of great interest to the War Department. Officials couldn't talk to John Surratt yet, but they knew where to find Mrs. Surratt and her daughter, Anna. And for good measure, the men wanted to question the boarders as well. Who knew what they might have seen or heard?

While detectives rounded up the boarders to take them in for questioning, a twenty-year-old man who called himself Lewis Paine appeared at the door. When the men asked him to explain why he was there, Paine replied that he was a laborer and that he had agreed to dig a gutter for Mrs. Surratt. He had come, he said, to find out when she wanted the job done.

One of the detectives turned to Mrs. Surratt and asked if she knew this man. Surratt barely glanced at Paine in the dark hall, then insisted that she had never seen him before. The men took Paine to headquarters for questioning, along with all the boarders, anyway.

Once at headquarters, the boarders took a closer look at Paine. One of them identified him as a friend of John Surratt's. This man, the boarder said, had used the name Reverend Wood before. Furthermore, he had spent several nights in the boardinghouse in March.

Because Paine's appearance matched the description of the intruder who attacked the Seward household, one of Seward's servants was brought to headquarters to look at the suspect. The servant identified Paine as the attacker. Paine was taken to the *Saugus*, one of two warships anchored nearby in the Potomac River. These ships were used as temporary prisons to make es-

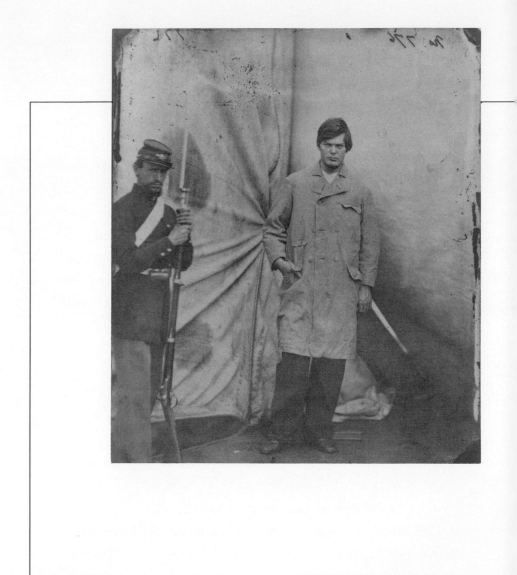

LEWIS PAINE

Lewis Paine, whose real name was Lewis Thornton Powell, was born in Alabama in either 1844 or 1845. He was one of ten children of George Powell, who became a Baptist minister when Lewis was three years old. After several moves, the family finally settled in Florida.

When Florida seceded from the Union, Lewis joined the Confederate Army. He was captured in 1863, but managed to escape and join Colonel John Mosby, who led raids against Union supporters in Virginia. While serving with Mosby, Lewis boarded at the Payne-Meredith home. He then changed his name to Payne, which he eventually spelled "Paine."

Lewis first met John Wilkes Booth backstage after a performance in Richmond during the war. They found that they shared a deep love for the Confederacy and each made a lasting impression on the other.

Paine regarded Booth as a hero, and after he left Mosby's raiders and moved north to Baltimore, he was deeply flattered when Booth recognized him when they chanced to meet on the street. By this time, Paine, unable to find work, was in desperate need of money. Booth was then in the early stages of organizing a kidnapping plot, and he needed co-conspirators. He offered to support Lewis. In return, Paine swore undying loyalty to the actor. *Photo courtesy of the Library of Congress.*

cape—or an attempted rescue—especially difficult. Shortly after, Arnold and O'Laughlin were taken on board. All three suspects were held in solitary confinement.

Certain that Mrs. Surratt had lied about Paine—and who knew what else?—officials locked her up in the Old Capitol Prison. This building, the temporary capitol after the British set fire to the real capitol during the War of 1812, was used to house Confederate spies during the Civil War.

When detectives found pictures of Booth hidden in Anna Surratt's room, she was also temporarily imprisoned, as were several other women in the house who admitted that they had met Booth. Such arrests would be illegal today. But during the war, President Lincoln had suspended the writ of *habeas corpus*, which until then had forced arresting officers to provide compelling proof that the suspect had committed a crime. The president suspended the writ for the duration of the war, a very unpopular act, so that officials could more easily arrest people thought to be Confederate agents. As a result, detectives and policemen were able to round up suspects at the mere hint of wrongdoing. Eventually the total number of people detained in the assassination case numbered in the hundreds.

Two days after Mrs. Surratt and her daughter were imprisoned, Edward Spangler was taken into custody. Spangler, about forty-three years old, had been a carpenter at the Booth estate in rural Maryland for many years. Booth was probably responsible for getting Spangler a job as a carpenter at Ford's Theatre. Jacob Ritterspaugh, a stagehand who had seen Booth ride off after the assassination, had rushed inside and told Spangler what he had

George Atzerodt supplemented his
income by ferrying Confederate
spies across the Potomac River. He
was brought into Booth's kidnapping plot by John Surratt, who had
often used his services. For a while,
Atzerodt lived in the Surratt boardinghouse. But when Mrs. Surratt
discovered that Atzerodt reeked of
tobacco and drank too much, she
told him to leave. Booth then put
up Atzerodt at a local hotel. *Photo
courtesy of the Library of Congress.*

Edward (also known as Edmund)
Spangler was a long-time friend of
Booth's. Spangler had worked as a
carpenter for Booth's father on the
family estate outside Baltimore
when Booth was a teenager.
Spangler, who had few friends,
idolized Booth. *Photo courtesy of the
Library of Congress.*

seen. Spangler, according to Ritterspaugh, had slapped him and told him to be quiet. When Ritterspaugh reported this to authorities, Spangler was arrested and charged with helping Booth escape. He, too, was taken to the *Saugus*.

The next day, George A. Atzerodt was arrested. Officials had learned from boarders in the Surratt house that Atzerodt was John's friend. Also, Atzerodt had stayed in the boardinghouse for a while in March, about the same time that Paine was there and Booth had visited often. It was then, officials guessed, that the murder plot had been hatched. In addition, Atzerodt had been seen in the Kirkwood House, where Vice President Andrew Johnson stayed, on the night of Lincoln's assassination. Officials wondered aloud if Atzerodt was supposed to kill Johnson.

It's not certain if detectives knew then that Atzerodt was part of the Confederate courier system. During the day he painted carriages, and at night he used one of several boats that he had hidden along the Potomac River to ferry Confederate couriers and spies between the Union and the Confederacy. John Surratt had been one of his best customers.

While detectives tried to find all the conspirators in the assassination plot, they were told about Booth's scheme to kidnap the president, a scheme that was, to say the least, fantastic. In late 1864, the North, which had a large population and an ample supply of soldiers, announced that it would no longer exchange prisoners of war. This had a drastic effect on the South, which needed every soldier it could muster. Booth then decided to capture Lincoln and take him to Richmond, where the Confederate government would hold him until all 35,000

Confederate prisoners of war were released. To finance this scheme, Booth sold his stock in an oil field in Pennsylvania, depositing the money in Canada, where he was reportedly seen talking to Confederate officials.

When Booth returned to Washington, he took steps to carry out his plan. He recruited his first accomplices, his old friends, Arnold and O'Laughlin, and scouted the countryside in southern Maryland for a practical route over which they could take the president. Although Maryland voted to remain loyal to the Union, as a slave state it had many Southern sympathizers. Booth carried at least one letter of introduction, a character recommendation from a Canadian official, and he used this letter to make the acquaintance of some of these Confederate supporters. Using the pretense of wanting to buy land, Booth traveled from one home to another without raising suspicion. One of the people he met in southern Maryland was Dr. William Queen, who then introduced him to Dr. Samuel A. Mudd, a thirty-one-year-old physician who owned a large estate. Dr. Mudd had some land to sell, and he offered to show Booth the parcel. Booth examined the acreage and spent one night at the doctor's home.

Booth saw Dr. Mudd again on December 23, 1864, while Mudd was visiting friends in Washington. The doctor knew the Surratt family, and, at Booth's request, he introduced the actor to John Surratt.

Booth knew of Surratt's support for the South, and he asked him to join the conspirators. Surratt not only agreed to do so, he bought Atzerodt into the plan, primarily because he could ferry the captured president across the river to Virginia. Surratt also recruited nineteen-year-old David Herold, an avid hunter who knew the back roads in southern Maryland very well.

Booth had planned to go to Richmond to see how his scheme would be received by Confederate officials. However, there is no proof that this happened.

The conspirators—Booth, Arnold, O'Laughlin, Paine, John Surratt, Atzerodt, and Herold—met as a group only one time in early or mid-March. Booth proposed that the men capture the president at Ford's Theatre, where he often attended plays. They would tie him up in his box, lower him to the stage, carry him out the back door to a waiting carriage, and race off to a boat at the Potomac River.

Booth's fellow conspirators were shocked when they heard the plan. How, they wanted to know, could they possibly hope to escape when there were literally hundreds of people around? Wouldn't at least one or two members of the audience give chase? they asked. And wouldn't the kidnappers be rather slow when trying to escape if they were carrying the president? The plan was ridiculous, they concluded, and they would not risk their lives for an attempt that was clearly doomed to failure. Even though Booth lost his temper and threatened the men if they didn't help him, not one of them agreed to do so.

So, Booth turned to a less dramatic scheme. On March 17, Lincoln was supposed to attend a play, *Still Waters Run Deep*, at the Campbell Hospital for soldiers, which was located a short distance from the capital. Booth suggested that the men kidnap Lincoln on a deserted stretch of the road. The conspirators agreed that this would be a more workable plan.

On the selected day, while Herold rented several horses at the local livery stable, the other men gathered their supplies, guns, ropes, and handcuffs (gear that Weichmann had seen in the boardinghouse), and, heady with anticipation, started toward the hospital. They stopped short, drank to their success, and waited for Lincoln to begin his journey back to Washington.

A little later, Booth rode ahead to see how the drama was progressing. He returned to his men shortly after, pale and shaken. The president had not attended the play. The men now feared that officials had gotten wind of their plot, and they ran for safety. Actually, Lincoln had simply changed his plans. Instead of attending the play, he had decided to visit with a Northern regiment in Washington that afternoon.

For all practical purposes, the kidnap plot was over. Booth assembled some of his men later that month, but the conspirators, especially Samuel Arnold, balked at another attempt. When Lincoln left the city, leaving Booth without a victim for a while, there was no more time to develop another plan. Nor was there any longer a need to exchange Lincoln for soldiers. General Lee's surrender on April 9 at the Appomattox Court House meant that the fighting was almost over.

War Department officials were skeptical at best that any kidnap scheme had actually existed. They thought that the prisoners were lying in a desperate attempt to explain their association with Booth. Being found guilty of conspiracy to kidnap might result in a prison term; being convicted of killing the president would most likely result in the death penalty. Officials would learn more about the alleged kidnapping plot when they arrested and questioned Booth. The problem was that no one knew exactly where he was at the moment. So to hasten an arrest, a reward was offered on April 20—$50,000 for the apprehension of Booth, $25,000 for the capture of John Surratt, and $25,000 for the arrest of David Herold. And in only a matter of days, men would lay claim to this reward. Two of the fugitives were about to be captured.

3 MORE ARRESTS

After John Wilkes Booth ran from Ford's Theatre, he made as rapid a getaway as possible, looking over his shoulder often as his horse charged through the alleys of Washington. But when Booth realized—to his great surprise—that no one was following him, he reined in his mare. For once, this actor wanted to avoid drawing attention to himself.

Booth's first destination was the Navy Yard bridge. This exit was guarded by Sergeant Silas T. Cobb. Immediately after Lincoln was shot, the secretary of war sent telegrams to the guards who were enforcing the curfew, warning them to be on the lookout for a killer. However, Cobb had not received this message. Therefore, he carried out his duties as usual, allowing individuals to leave or enter the capital after the deadline as long as they did not appear to be troublemakers.

Booth played his part at the bridge very well. Outwardly, he was calm and relaxed, and he made no attempt to disguise him-

The Navy Yard bridge was guarded by the only soldier who had not been told to be on the lookout for assassins. John Wilkes Booth crossed this bridge on his escape route out of Washington. David Herold crossed here a few minutes later. *Photo courtesy of the Library of Congress.*

self, giving the sergeant his real name when asked for identification. Booth explained that he had been delayed on business, otherwise he never would have arrived so late. Now he simply wanted to go to his home, which, he said, was just across the bridge. Cobb believed him and allowed the assassin to leave the city.

About fifteen minutes later, David Herold approached Cobb. He, too, convinced the guard to allow him to cross the bridge.

Shortly after, John Fletcher arrived at Cobb's station, his horse in a lather. Fletcher worked at the livery stable where Herold had rented a horse that day. Herold had failed to return the mount on time. When Fletcher spotted him heading toward the outskirts of town, the liveryman believed, correctly, that Herold had no intention of bringing the horse back. Now Fletcher was in hot pursuit of the stable's property. Cobb thought that this rider behaved in a suspicious manner, and although the guard said that he would allow Fletcher to pass, he would not allow him to return that evening.

Fletcher swung around in anger and headed toward the police station to report the missing horse. But the police, who at this point did not know that Herold was a friend of Booth's, were far too busy looking for conspirators to take time to hunt down a horse thief.

Herold caught up with Booth a few miles south of the capital. Herold's assignment that night was to guide Lewis Paine, who was unfamiliar with the streets of Washington, to William Seward's home. There he was to wait for Paine to kill the secretary of state, and then guide Paine to a meeting place with Booth and Atzerodt, who was, as officials had guessed, supposed to kill Vice President Johnson. Once the group had assembled, Herold would lead it through a maze of back roads to Atzerodt's boat at Port Tobacco. The men had planned to cross the Potomac River at this port, enter Virginia, and receive a hero's welcome.

Booth immediately questioned Herold about Paine's success. Herold did not know the outcome. He had panicked, he said, when the assault did not go as easily as planned, and people in

David Herold, like George Atzerodt, was introduced to Booth by John Surratt. Surratt had relied on him in the past to help him get past pickets and guards when he was working as a spy. Herold was the youngest of the conspirators, and according to his lawyer, easily led astray. *Photo courtesy of the Library of Congress.*

the Seward household began to throw open their windows and cry for help. Afraid of getting caught, Herold had fled, leaving Paine on his own.

Booth and Herold proceeded to Surratt's tavern. Here they picked up a rifle, a field glass, and some whiskey from John Lloyd and waited briefly for Paine and Atzerodt. When neither arrived on time, Booth and Herold went on by themselves.

By now, Booth's leg was extremely painful, and he was forced to seek medical help as soon as possible. Instead of going directly to Colonel Samuel Cox's home as planned, Booth and Herold decided to see Dr. Samuel Mudd. Booth had made no attempt to disguise himself while committing his crime or making his escape and, according to John Lloyd, had openly bragged about shooting the president while he was in Surratt's tavern. Now he chose to try to conceal his identity. Both Dr. Mudd and his wife, Frances, would later insist that Booth had worn a false beard and had pulled his cloak up to his ears, covering most of his face.

The men arrived at Dr. Mudd's home about 4:00 A.M. on April 15. After awakening the doctor from a deep sleep, Herold told him that he had a friend outside who had fallen from his horse. His friend was in severe pain, Herold said, and he needed medical attention.

Dr. Mudd agreed to examine the patient. The doctor helped Booth into the house and told Herold to take him to an upstairs bedroom. When Mudd tried to pull Booth's boot off a now badly swollen leg so that he could examine it, the actor cried out in pain. Mudd then cut the boot to remove it, tossing it aside. He treated the fracture, making a temporary splint from hat boxes, and ordered Booth to rest. Meanwhile, the doctor told one of his servants to make a crutch for Booth, so that he might get around a little easier.

That afternoon, Dr. Mudd went into Bryantown. Here he learned that President Lincoln had been assassinated. It was also in Bryantown that Mudd encountered the first of more than seven thousand troops who would soon arrive. War Department officials had questioned guards at all exits from Washington, eventually learning that two men, Booth and possibly an ac-complice, had crossed the Navy Yard bridge. After talking to Lloyd, who was arrested, the agents knew for certain that they were looking for two men who were heading toward Virginia. They believed that Booth and Herold were now somewhere in

Dr. Samuel Mudd, a Marylander, was the son of a wealthy landowner. When questioned about helping Booth, Mudd gave incredible accounts of what had happened. Historians have long wondered why he lied, for he certainly lied. Most believe that he was trying to protect his family; others believe that he had something to hide. Whatever his reason, his falsehoods nearly cost him his life. Mudd, who had been a friend of the Surratt family, had introduced Booth to John Surratt, Jr. *Photo courtesy of the Library of Congress.*

southern Maryland, hidden away by some of the many Southern sympathizers in the area.

Shortly after Mudd returned home, Herold insisted that he and his friend had to leave soon. Herold asked for directions for a shortcut through Zekiah Swamp, put Booth on his horse, and started off into the wilderness.

The trail was poorly marked, and by nightfall the men were lost. They tried to find a way out of the thicket on Easter Sunday, but they were unable to do so. Hungry and exhausted—they had to walk through the tangled mess, no easy task for Booth—they finally stumbled upon the home of Oswald

Swann, a former slave who lived on the edge of the wetland. Swann agreed to help the men, leading them to Colonel Cox's home.

Everyone now knew about the massive manhunt, and they understood the great risk one took by helping the fugitives. Even so, Cox would not turn his back on Booth and Herold. Whether Cox allowed the men to enter his home is not clear, and if they did so, they did not remain long. Instead, shortly after arriving, Booth and Herold were led to a spot in a nearby woods. They were to hide here until they could be taken to a boat on the Potomac River.

For six days, the two men camped in a thicket as soldiers, detectives, and reward-seekers looked for them. Afraid that their horses would whinny and give them away—detectives once passed within two hundred feet of their hiding place—Herold led the horses some distance from their campsite and killed them.

As soon as Booth and Herold were secreted away, Cox contacted Thomas A. Jones, a relative who had routinely smuggled letters between Richmond and Washington during the war. Many of these letters contained military secrets, and Jones had been arrested by Union soldiers at least once for his activities. Cox, who told Jones what the fugitives had done, asked him to lead them to the river as soon as it was safe to do so.

Jones furnished the men with food and newspapers while they waited. Booth not only wanted to read reports about his activities, he was seeking information about Paine and Atzerodt and looking for a two-page letter that he had written on April

THOMAS A. JONES'S ACCOUNT

Thomas A. Jones helped Booth and Herold. Many years later, when it was safe to do so, he described his activities.

I heard of the murder of President Lincoln on Saturday afternoon, April 15, 1865.

The next day a young man came to me from Samuel Cox's house. [He said] that Booth and his companion were secreted in a thicket of dense pines about a mile from the house. Cox said I must get Booth and his companion, whom I afterward learned was Herold, across the river. I consented . . . and started out to find their hiding place.

Booth . . . was lying on the ground wrapt in a blanket. A crutch [obtained at Dr. Mudd's home] was lying by his side and his foot was bandaged. His face was pallid and drawn, as if he was worn with pain and anxiety. . . . He was abrupt in his questioning, and about the first sentence he uttered was to inquire what people had to say of his crime. He asked me to get him some newspapers, which I did. He frankly admitted that he was the murderer of the president and expressed no regret for the act. We then discussed ways and means of getting himself and Herold across the river, and where he could get necessary medical attention. As the country was overrun with federal soldiers, it was decided that Booth was to remain where he was until a more favorable opportunity for escape was presented.

Had I desired it, I could have got $100,000 for betraying Booth, as that amount was offered in my presence by an officer of the federal government. I was then a ruined man financially, but the thought of betraying him never once entered my mind for a single instant.[6]

14, only hours before he shot Lincoln. In this letter, Booth had listed his reasons for committing the assassination. He had given the document to John Mathews, a fellow actor, after making Mathews promise to deliver the envelope to the *National Intelligencer*, a newspaper in Washington, the following day. However, after learning that Booth had shot Lincoln, Mathews had feared that just having the letter might somehow incriminate him, so he had burned it. So, Booth did not see his words in print. Instead of blaming Mathews, Booth thought that the government had censored him. Worse yet for Booth, who expected words of praise, editors called him a cutthroat and a coward, even in the South.

On Sunday, the day after the fugitives left, Mudd sought advice from George Mudd, his cousin. The doctor told George about the two strangers who had visited his home. He was afraid that they might be the men the soldiers were seeking. If Mudd told the soldiers about the strangers and they turned out to be the assassin and his accomplice, Mudd was afraid that he would be arrested for helping them. Would it be better, he wondered aloud, if he said nothing at all? Mudd's cousin insisted that the doctor talk to the soldiers. Someone might have seen the strangers at Mudd's home or the servants might mention the late-night visitors. Then, George argued, Mudd would be in even more trouble, for it would appear as if he knew who the men were and was withholding information to help them escape. Mudd's cousin offered to approach the soldiers, several of whom he knew, on Mudd's behalf. He did so on Monday, April 17.

On Tuesday, soldiers questioned the doctor. Mudd insisted

that he didn't know who the strangers were, and when shown a picture of Booth, Mudd insisted that the man he treated was not the actor. Although Mudd believed that the interview went well, the commanding officer thought that the doctor was withholding information.

As a result, the soldiers returned again on April 21. This time Mudd was taken in for questioning after the soldiers found a boot beneath the bed where Mudd had treated his mysterious stranger. Inside the boot was the name "John Wilkes." Mudd, understandably rattled, gave confusing and incredible answers during his second interview. Even so, the officers released him.

On April 24, however, soldiers, now convinced that the doctor was involved in a plot with Booth, arrested Mudd. They took him to the Old Capitol Prison in Washington.

By this time, Booth and Herold were in Virginia. Led by Thomas Jones, the men had begun to make their way out of the woods late in the afternoon on April 21. Some soldiers thought that they had spotted Booth in nearby St. Mary's County that day. After Jones was certain that most of the troops were headed there, he had rushed to the woods, collected the fugitives, and started a dangerous trek to his boat. At the riverfront, he gave Herold directions and bid the men farewell.

But the wind and tide were against the men, and instead of landing on the opposite shore, they were pushed back to Maryland. Herold recognized the landing spot, and he sought help from an acquaintance, John Hughes, who successfully helped the men reach Virginia.

Booth relied on the people he had contacted while putting

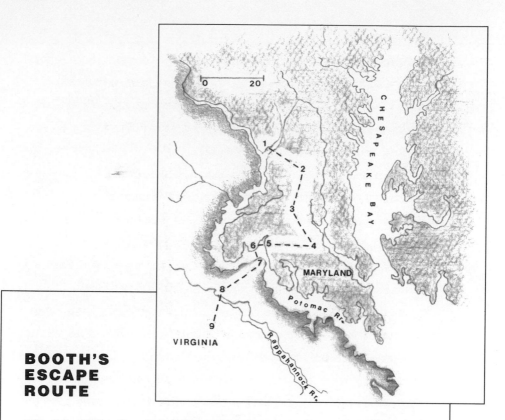

BOOTH'S ESCAPE ROUTE

After John Wilkes Booth fled Washington, D.C. (**1** on the map), he traveled to Surrattsville (**2**), where he was joined by David Herold. They picked up a gun and some liquor at Mary Surratt's tavern before going on to Dr. Samuel Mudd's home (**3**). After receiving medical care from Dr. Mudd, Booth and Herold took a shortcut through Zekiah Swamp (**3-4**). They became hopelessly lost, and upon arriving at the home of Oswald Swann (**4**), they asked for help. Swann took them to Colonel Samuel Cox's home (**5**), where they hid in the woods for five days. Booth and Herold then tried to cross the Potomac River, but were blown back to Maryland's shore (**6**). They eventually reached Virginia (**7**) and with help from a number of Confederates, managed to reach Port Conway (**8**), where they took a ferry across the Rappahannock River. Later they were captured at Garrett's farm (**9**). *Map courtesy of Karen Zeinert.*

together his kidnapping plot to help him escape from federal troops. In addition, he still carried the letter of introduction written by a Confederate in Canada so that he could make new contacts should he need more help. He received aid from a surprising number of people, although it was often given grudgingly. His contacts included Mrs. Elizabeth Quesenberry, Thomas Harbin, William Bryant, and Dr. Richard Stuart.

After leaving Stuart's property, Booth and Herold decided to pretend that they were Confederate soldiers. They hired a former slave to take them to a ferry landing on the Rappahannock River, arriving sometime in the morning of April 24.

At the landing, Herold approached three soldiers who were on their way home, Captain Willie Jett, Major Mortimer Ruggles, and Lieutenant Absalom Bainbridge. Herold asked them if he and his companion, who, Herold said, had been wounded in the war, might travel with them. When the men resisted, Herold confessed that he was traveling with John Wilkes Booth, the assassin. The soldiers, after a lengthy discussion among themselves, finally agreed to help.

Once across the river, the soldiers put Booth on one of their horses, and led him from one place to another to try to find someone who would take him in. This proved to be a very difficult task. It is not clear if the people who were approached knew who Booth and Herold were, or if they simply didn't want to house strangers. In any case, it was not the hero's welcome that Booth had envisioned. Finally, the conspirators were taken to the home of Richard H. Garrett, where the men eventually ended up staying in the tobacco barn.

While soldiers continued to look for the conspirators, War Department detectives had been given a clue that made capture certain. By this time, the manhunt was being led almost entirely by Colonel Lafayette C. Baker. He received word that two men who matched Booth's and Herold's descriptions had been seen in a boat near Port Tobacco. Baker immediately sent twenty-five cavalrymen under Lieutenant Edward P. Doherty's command and two of the government's best detectives, Colonel Everton I. Conger and Lieutenant Luther Byron Baker, to the port.

After questioning the witness, the men headed south, arriving at the Rappahannock ferry twenty-four hours after Booth had been there. Not only did the ferryman recognize pictures of the fugitives, he knew one of the soldiers who crossed with Booth, Captain Jett. Better yet, the ferryman knew where the detectives could find Jett; he was visiting his girlfriend in nearby Bowling Green.

So the detectives rushed to Bowling Green. Eager to capture Booth and testy from lack of sleep, the men lost little time on niceties. They barged in on the captain, dragged him out of bed, and threatened him by holding a gun to his head. Jett had little choice but to cooperate, and he agreed to lead the men to Garrett's farm.

They arrived at 2:00 A.M. on April 26. Lieutenant Baker, in more of a hurry than ever, pounded on Garrett's door, demanding that the owner open it immediately. Upon questioning, Mr. Garrett said that the men they wanted were somewhere in the woods. Baker doubted this, and he gave Garrett one more chance to tell him where Booth and Herold were. If Garrett re-

BOOTH'S DIARY

John Wilkes Booth kept a diary. Although this was taken from him when he was captured, it was not mentioned publicly until nearly two years later. Then, when produced, it was missing eighteen pages. This controversial diary sheds light on Booth's beliefs and feelings. The entries below were written while he was being hunted down, even though the first has a date of April 13, the day before the assassination.

April 13, 14
For six months we had worked to capture. But our cause [the Confederacy's independence] being almost lost, something decisive and great must be done.

I struck boldly [on April 14], and not as the papers say. I walked with a firm step through a thousand of his friends. . . . A Colonel was at his side. . . . In jumping, broke my leg. I passed all his pickets. Rode sixty miles last night, with the bone of my leg tearing the flesh at every jump.

I can never repent it though we hated to kill. Our country owed all our troubles to him, and God simply made me the instrument of his punishment.

fused to do so, Baker said that he would hang him. While one of the soldiers began to prepare a noose, one of Garrett's sons intervened, admitting that the men Baker sought were in the barn.

A few cavalrymen watched the house; the rest headed toward and then surrounded the outbuilding. When Garrett's second son joined the soldiers, Baker pushed him toward the barn and

April 1865

I care not what becomes of me. I have no desire to out live my country.

April 21

After being hunted like a dog . . . with everyman's hand against me, I am here in despair. And why? I, for striking down a . . . tyrant . . . am looked upon as a common cut-throat. . . . I hoped for no gain. I knew no private wrong. I struck for my country and that alone. A country that groaned beneath this tyranny, and prayed for this end, and yet now behold the cold hand they extend to me. . . . The little, the very little I left behind to clear my name [the letter he had given Mathews], the government will not allow to be printed. So ends all. For my country I have given up all that makes life sweet and holy [and] brought misery upon my family. . . . Tonight I will once more try the river with the intent to cross. Though I have a great desire and almost a mind to return to Washington, and in a measure clear my name—which I feel I can do. I do not repent the blow I struck. I may before my God, but not to man. I think I have done well.

Who can read his fate? God's will be done. I have too great a soul to die like a criminal. . . . I do not wish to shed a drop of blood, but "I must fight the course!" 'Tis all that's left me.[7]

demanded that he go inside and get the fugitives' weapons. The young man was met with stiff resistance from Booth, who called the son a traitor, among other things, and threatened to kill him if he didn't leave.

The son reported his failure to Baker, who responded by demanding that the fugitives surrender. After only a few minutes,

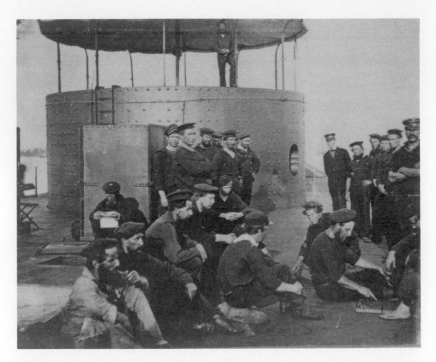

The *Saugus* was one of two vessels used to house the assassination suspects. (The other was the *Montauk*.) These ships were heavily armed monitors that could be moved if necessary, and were thought by the War Department to be more secure than a prison. The suspects were photographed on the monitor (note the metal background in some of their photographs), and then chained and held in separate compartments. *Photo courtesy of the Library of Congress.*

Herold agreed to do so. He approached the front of the barn and stuck out his empty hands. Baker grabbed him and passed him on to other soldiers who tied him to a tree. Booth, however, refused to give up. He told the soldiers that he would die first. To force him out, Baker set fire to the barn. Even though flames shot high into the air and then raced toward Booth, he refused to come out. Instead, he picked up his rifle and began to take aim. Suddenly a shot rang out, and Booth dropped to the floor. Sergeant Boston Corbett, disobeying orders to bring Booth in alive, had fired at the fugitive, fatally wounding him in the neck.

Booth was dragged from the burning barn by Baker and Conger and taken to Garrett's front porch. He died there several hours later, after asking soldiers to tell his mother that he had died for his country.

Soldiers wrapped Booth's body in a blanket, loaded it onto a buggy, and started for the Potomac River. Herold walked behind. They were taken to the *Montauk*, one of the warships serving as a temporary prison for assassination suspects. They arrived in the morning of April 27. Herold was taken below and put in solitary confinement. Soldiers handcuffed him and chained a fifty-pound lead ball to one of his ankles. Like the other prisoners now, he was forced to wear a heavy cotton hood that made communication with anyone impossible. Booth's body lay on the deck until late afternoon.

Shortly before sundown, in full view of a growing crowd that lined the riverbank, Colonel Baker and Lieutenant Baker put Booth's body and some heavy chains aboard a small boat and headed toward a swamp near Geeseborough Point. The men made it appear as if Booth's body was to be sunk in the swamp's slimy depths, where old mules and dead army horses had been "buried" for years.

When it was pitch black, the boat, still carrying Booth's corpse, proceeded to a nearby penitentiary located on the grounds of an old arsenal. Booth's body was removed from the boat and buried beneath the prison floor. Union officials were not about to use any public burial site where mourners might gather and shed a tear for the assassin. And somehow this site seemed most fitting, for those accused of being his co-conspirators were about to be tried in this very building.

4 ON TRIAL

While souvenir seekers looked for Booth's body in the swamp and only two weeks after Lincoln had been assassinated, Secretary of War Stanton wrapped up his investigation of the president's murder. Most of Stanton's information had been gathered by General Joseph Holt, who was the head of the Bureau of Military Justice. In addition to building an airtight case against Arnold, O'Laughlin, Spangler, Atzerodt, Herold, Paine, Mudd, and Mary Surratt, Holt had located some eyewitnesses who said that they could prove that the Confederacy was behind the murder. On May 1, Holt gave his information to Secretary Stanton, who passed it on to President Johnson.

On May 2, Johnson identified Jefferson Davis and other Confederate officials and advisors as the men responsible for Lincoln's death. He said:

It appears from evidence in the Bureau of Military Justice that the atrocious murder of the late President Abraham Lincoln and the attempted assassination of the Honorable William H. Seward, Secretary of State, were incited, concerted, and procured by Jefferson Davis, Jacob Thompson, Clement C. Clay, Beverly Tucker, George Sanders, and William C. Cleary. Now, therefore, to the end that justice may be done, I, Andrew Johnson, President of the United States, do offer and promise [rewards] for the arrest of said persons . . . so that they can be brought to trial.[8]

The rewards being offered were large: $100,000 for Davis; $25,000 each for Clay, Thompson, Sanders, and Tucker; and $10,000 for Cleary.

Until this announcement was made, cabinet members and War Department officials had held heated debates about where to try the prisoners, in a civil courtroom or in a military court. Now that the department had proof of a Confederate conspiracy, Holt argued that the assassination was not only murder, it was an act of war. Since other Union civilians involved in Confederate conspiracies had been tried in military courts during the war, Holt said that these suspects should be tried there as well.

Attorney General James Speed agreed with Holt. Besides, eager for conviction, he knew that holding a military trial would offer four advantages to the War Department. First, a military court would provide a quick hearing. A special commission would be chosen immediately to listen to the charges, avoiding the usual delay of waiting until one's case came up before a civil court. This would please the public, which was clamoring for action. Second, the rules of evidence in a military court were not as strict as those in a civil court, making conviction easier. Third, the prisoners could be tried as a group. This meant that the evidence used against one suspect could apply to all of them, making the prosecution's burden much lighter. And finally, military procedure limited the number of appeals that could be made. So a conviction, if obtained, would not easily be overturned.

On May 6, the commission of nine men who would hear the case was announced. The members were high-ranking military officers, some of whom were war heroes. This panel was led by Major General David Hunter, a close friend of Lincoln's and one of the mourners on the funeral train. He had rushed back to Washington from Lincoln's last service in Springfield to serve on the panel.

The War Department also announced the names of the three judge advocates on May 6. They would present the department's case. General Holt, who had secured so much of the evidence, would be the leader of the advocates. He would be assisted by Brevet Colonel H.L. Burnett, well known for his prosecution of civilians in military courts, and John Bingham, a member of the House of Representatives, a powerful and persuasive speaker.

While the commission was being organized, the prisoners were taken to the penitentiary where Booth was buried. The men who had been kept aboard the warships were still hooded,

The military commission that tried and judged the assassination suspects is shown here. The nine-member jury included, left to right: David R. Clendenin, C.H. Tomkins, Thomas M. Harris, Albion P. Howe, James A. Ekin, Lew Wallace, David Hunter, August V. Kautz, and Robert S. Foster. The two judge advocates are shown next. They are John A. Bingham (seated behind the table) and Henry L. Burnett, standing behind the table. Joseph Holt, the judge advocate general and main prosecutor, is at the far right. *Photo courtesy of the Library of Congress.*

shackled, and limited in their movements by fifty-pound balls chained to their ankles. The prisoners shuffled along the best they could, while soldiers carried their weights, separating and guiding the men as they inched along to their cells. Dr. Mudd and Mrs. Surratt were brought to the prison in separate carriages under heavy guard. Once inside his cell, Mudd was chained and given a hood to wear.

Brevet Major General John F. Hartranft was in charge of the conspirators, and he made sure that escape was nearly impossible. Even if the prisoners, with balls and chains in tow, escaped from their individual cells and the two guards who stood before each one and somehow managed to climb over the twenty-five-foot wall that surrounded the prison, cavalrymen who could give chase stood ready at all times. If someone tried to rescue the prisoners, they would face a barrage of artillery, for Hartranft had surrounded the prison with cannons.

The first three days of the trial, May 9-11, were spent on establishing rules for the hearing and swearing in lawyers for the defense. These men were an impressive lot, and considering the public's animosity toward the suspects, it took great courage on the lawyers' part to defend the prisoners. The principal spokesmen were: Walter S. Cox, a Washington lawyer with many years of experience; Thomas Ewing, Jr., a Union general and former chief justice of the Supreme Court of Kansas; Frederick Stone, an attorney in Port Tobacco and a family friend of the Herolds'; William E. Doster, a former provost marshal of Washington, D.C.; Reverdy Marshall, a U.S. senator from Maryland and an expert on the U.S. Constitution; and Marshall's assistants, Frederick W. Aiken and John W. Clampitt.

On May 10, the eight prisoners, with hoods removed, filed into the room to hear the charges against them. First, the prisoners were accused of conspiring with a slew of Confederate officials to murder President Lincoln, Vice President Johnson, Secretary of State Seward, and General Grant—a very serious offense. Then all eight were charged with putting their plan into motion, a crime punishable by death.

The same day that the prisoners were charged, another suspect, Confederate president Jefferson Davis, was captured.

When Jefferson Davis became the President of the Confederate States of America in 1861, he was an experienced politician. Davis had been elected to Congress in 1845, where he represented Mississippi. He resigned shortly after to lead a volunteer regiment in the Mexican War. Davis then returned to Congress in 1847. In 1853, he became President Franklin Pierce's secretary of war, and it was during this period that he successfully laid plans for a transcontinental railroad to link California to the East Coast. After Pierce left office, Davis returned to the Senate but resigned again when Mississippi seceded. He hoped to become chief commander of the Southern army—he was a graduate of West Point and a military hero—but instead was asked to be the South's president. *Photo courtesy of the Library of Congress.*

President Davis and his cabinet had abandoned Richmond after loading the Confederacy's records and treasury onto wagons on April 2. Even though federal troops had entered the capital the next day and were pushing farther south every moment, Davis had refused to believe that his cause was lost. Instead, as he and other officials had headed toward safer ground, he had talked about moving the government across the Mississippi River.

Meanwhile, his wife, Varina, had taken flight. Believing the worst of the North, Davis had been afraid of what might happen to her and their four children should they be caught by federal troops. With an escort of Confederate soldiers, she had traveled through long stretches of wilderness to try to reach the Gulf Coast of Florida. There she had hoped to make arrangements to sail to England.

President Davis had eventually learned that thieves were looking for the Confederacy's gold in the very area in Georgia where Varina and the children were thought to be at that time. Davis had then followed his wife's trail southward, locating her on May 7. They had traveled together for several days, trying to stay ahead of both bandits and federal troops.

Late at night on May 10, near Irwinville, the Davises' flight had come to an abrupt end. It had rained all day, and the Davises and their escorts, after slogging through mud for hours, were exhausted. While they slept soundly, three hundred Union soldiers surrounded their camp. Davis was arrested and charged with procuring the murder of Lincoln, a charge he forcefully denied.

Davis was taken to Fort Monroe, near Richmond, to await

trial. Here he joined Clement Clay, a close friend and advisor, who was also charged with Lincoln's murder. Clay had surrendered himself to stand trial shortly after Johnson's announcement on May 2. He was as defiant and indignant as Davis. Murder, indeed!

Needless to say, Stanton and Holt were happy to have at least two Confederate leaders in prison, especially President Davis. Both department officials hoped that these latest prisoners might provide more evidence to use against the eight suspects on trial. And, of course, there would be trials later for the Confederate leaders. Justice, in Stanton's opinion, was at hand.

On May 12, defense lawyers began their struggle to save their clients' lives. Before a hushed crowd, the attorneys asked that the trial be moved to a civil court. When the panel refused to grant this request, defense lawyers asked the commission to try the eight prisoners separately. This request was also denied. The attorneys then announced that their clients were not guilty, which would force the prosecution to prove its case. The audience took a deep breath, leaned forward for the best view possible, and waited for the arguments to start.

The prosecution's case consisted of three parts, the first of which was to present witnesses who would prove that the assaults were a Confederate plot. The first witness to testify was Richard Montgomery, a Union spy in Canada. Montgomery said that he had been told by several members of the Canadian cabinet that the South had friends all over the North who were prepared to kill Lincoln, Stanton, Grant, and a few others, as soon as they were given the word to do so. One of the men cabinet officers had talked to was none other than John Wilkes Booth, who had made at least three trips to Montreal to discuss the assassinations in detail.

Montgomery's testimony was backed by Sanford Conover. He had been part of the Confederate War Department in Richmond until 1863, when he moved to Canada. Conover testified that he knew all the members of the Richmond and Canadian cabinets very well, especially Jacob Thompson (who was on President Johnson's wanted list). Conover said that Thompson told him about Booth's plan. Furthermore, Conover insisted that he was in Thompson's office when John Surratt arrived with messages about an assassination plot from President Davis. According to Conover, Thompson read the letters, smiled, and said, "This makes the thing all right."[9]

The commission was impressed with these witnesses, even though some citizens called the men habitual liars. The panel ignored the name-callers, however, believing that they were part of a plot to save Davis.

After presenting evidence to establish a Confederate tie, the prosecutors moved to the second part of their case. They argued that from the beginning, the prisoners had planned to commit murder. The prosecutors admitted that they had been told about a kidnapping plot and that murder had been discussed only after the first plot failed. However, the judge advocates found it impossible to believe this.

Prosecutor Bingham was the most effective in raising questions about the kidnapping scheme. Concentrating only on the plan to hog-tie Lincoln in the theatre, Bingham was barely able to keep a straight face when he described the plot to the commission. No one, Bingham said, not even Booth, would propose such a scheme.

To further support their argument that murder was Booth's intention all along, the prosecutors presented witness after witness who had long before heard Booth mutter something about killing Lincoln. In addition, three witnesses, including two policemen, testified that a man answering Booth's description had tried to break through a line of guards who were protecting Lincoln during his second inauguration ceremony on March 4, 1865. These men now believed that Booth had planned to assassinate Lincoln then and there. Interestingly enough, Booth's diary, in which he stated that he had tried for months to capture the president, was never mentioned in the trial.

When the prosecutors believed that they had shown beyond a reasonable doubt that Davis and Booth were in cahoots in a long-standing murder plot, the three advocates turned their attention to the third part of their case, prosecuting the eight prisoners. Because the suspects were being tried as one, there was no attempt to take testimony in any particular order. This caused great confusion among the spectators, as did the sheer number of witnesses. More than three hundred people took the stand between May 12 and June 14.

The evidence against David Herold was overwhelming, and prosecutors had little difficulty proving that he was part of the assassination plot. He had been caught with Booth, and witnesses had placed him near Seward's house on the night of April 14. Defense lawyers tried to show that the suspect was childish and easily led. It was a weak defense, but it was the best that they could do.

Lewis Paine's situation was equally difficult. Several witnesses had seen him attack Seward. Mr. Doster, who defended Paine, tried to plead insanity for his client. He argued that Paine himself, after attacking Seward, had shouted, "I'm mad! I'm mad!"[10] In addition, Paine's behavior in court was not normal. Unlike the other prisoners, he entered the room with his head held high, and he paid little attention to anyone's testimony. Doster concluded that Paine really didn't understand what was happening. Likewise, he hadn't really understood what he was doing when he tried to kill Seward. The prosecutors sneered, then produced several doctors who, after talking to Paine, insisted that he understood perfectly well what he had done.

George Atzerodt admitted that he had conspired with Booth, but his crime, he insisted, was only that of planning to kidnap— nothing more. Because the prisoners were not allowed to testify, attorney Doster read a statement to the commission that was written by Atzerodt.

On the evening of the 14th of April, I met Booth and Paine at the Herndon House, in this city at eight o'clock. He (Booth) said he himself would murder Mr. Lincoln and General Grant, Paine should take Mr. Seward, and I should take Mr. Johnson. I told him I would not do it; that I had gone into the thing to capture, but I was not going to kill. He told me I was a fool . . . that it was death for every man who backed out; and so we parted. I wandered about the streets until about two o'clock in the morning, and . . . [eventually] went to my cousin's house, in Montgomery County, where I was arrested.[11]

The prosecution refused to accept this story. Instead, it produced witnesses who testified that Atzerodt had for some time been asking questions about the vice president's daily schedule. Surely, prosecutors argued, this had nothing to do with the imaginary kidnapping plot of Lincoln. It proved that Atzerodt had long before planned to kill Johnson. Besides, prosecutors added, Booth had certainly made up his mind before that night, since he had been in the theatre early that day to find a brace and to drill a hole in the door of the presidential box. In addition, even if Atzerodt had refused to participate rather than simply failing to find his victim, which was what prosecutors thought had happened, why hadn't Atzerodt warned government officials? He had lots of time to do so. The defense lawyers had no reply. Atzerodt was in serious trouble.

Samuel Arnold had implicated himself and his friend Michael O'Laughlin in the letter signed "Sam," which was found in Booth's room after the assassination. Since the prosecution refused to believe in a kidnapping plot, the judge advocates argued that the letter was proof positive that the men were in on the murder plot. However, the prosecution could not place either man at the murder scene, nor could anyone prove that the men had helped Booth on April 14. O'Laughlin had been with friends on the night that Lincoln was killed, and the suspect could prove it. Even so, the men were linked to the plot, and as a result, they were only steps away from the gallows.

Edward Spangler, the stagehand, had been arrested because he supposedly told another crew member not to tell which direction Booth had taken after leaving the theatre. At the trial, new charges were leveled at Booth's old friend. Witnesses testified that he held the back door open for Booth on the night of the assassination, then held it shut so that the men who tried to follow Booth were stopped just long enough for the murderer to escape. But Spangler had not been involved in the kidnapping plot, and since prosecutors were using this list of conspirators for its murder suspects, the prosecution couldn't prove that Spangler was part of Booth's murder plot. Therefore, he had a fighting chance to save his life.

In order to tie Samuel Mudd to the plot, prosecutors had to call many witnesses to the stand. Former slaves testified that Mudd was a Southerner at heart, who hid Confederate couriers in his woods. They also said that Mudd had associated with Mrs. Surratt's husband, who routinely harbored Confederate spies. Next, the soldiers who had questioned Mudd said that the doctor had withheld information and had refused to identify Booth as his mysterious patient until Booth was out of their reach. Louis Weichmann, a boarder at the Surratt house and now a key witness for the government, testified that he was present when Mudd introduced John Surratt to Booth on December 23 in Washington. That same evening, Weichmann recalled, Mudd and Booth had held private conversations and had drawn what looked like a map on an envelope.

From the time that he was arrested, for reasons known only to Mudd, he had insisted that he hadn't seen Booth in Washington on December 23. This lie seriously undermined his defense. Although his lawyers produced friends, neighbors, and former slaves to prove that Mudd was a decent, law-abiding citizen who was only doing his professional duty when he helped Booth, this testimony fell on deaf ears. Even the fact that some of the witnesses who testified against Mudd were proved to be liars did little to help him. Mudd was in serious trouble.

The case against Mary Surratt was built from the testimony of Weichmann and John Lloyd, who, like Weichmann, was now a government witness. After prosecutors listed the conspirators who had stayed at the boardinghouse and wondered aloud how Mrs. Surratt could claim that she didn't know that something was going on, the advocates put Weichmann on the stand. He testified that Mary had held many hushed conversations with Booth when he visited and that she had talked to him on the morning of the assassination.

Lloyd told the commission that Mary, who had been driven to his tavern by Louis Weichmann on April 14, the day of the assassination, had delivered a message and a package for Booth. Lloyd was to have two guns, which John Surratt had hidden in the tavern, a field glass, and whiskey ready for Booth to pick up that night. How, prosecutors asked, could Mary have known Booth's escape route if she wasn't part of the plot?

Detectives added to the case against Surratt. They described the arrival of Paine at her home on April 17 and her insistence that she had never seen the man before, which was not true. The fact that Paine had turned to her after wandering about for several days was proof that she was part of the plot, they added. Why else would he have trusted her with his life?

The defense struggled hard to overcome the prosecution's arguments. The lawyers produced testimony about Mary's character. All of these witnesses said that she had been an upstanding woman who worked hard, helped her neighbors, and went to Mass regularly. She was not the type of person who would support a plot to murder the president or anyone else, for that matter.

Next, her lawyers defended her actions. The fact that so many of the accused had roomed at her boardinghouse was not Mrs. Surratt's doing, the men said, it was her son's. And hushed conversations, the lawyers added, proved nothing. Her decision to deliver a message and a package for Booth to Lloyd, if indeed she did so, were simply acts of kindness. She was going there anyway to meet with a business acquaintance. The fact that she failed to recognize Paine was due to her poor eyesight. Even the boarders, the lawyers pointed out, did not immediately recognize him, for Paine was disheveled and wore a strange cap unlike any the boarders had ever seen. (His hat was cut from a sleeve of his undershirt. He had lost his hat at the Seward home, and, believing that not wearing something on his head in public would draw more attention to him than wearing a silly hat would, he made one from what he had on hand.) Like Mudd's defense, Surratt's fell on deaf ears.

After listening to weeks of testimony, the commission deliberated nearly two weeks before reaching its verdicts. Spangler was found not guilty of conspiracy. However, since he helped Booth, the panel recommended that he be sentenced to six years in prison. The rest were found guilty of conspiracy, and because three (Booth, Paine, and Herold) had clearly been involved in murder and attempted murder, all who had been connected to the plot were convicted of participating in murder to some degree. Therefore, the punishments were harsh. Arnold, O'Laughlin, and Mudd were to be imprisoned for the rest of their lives. Paine, Atzerodt, Herold, and Mary Surratt were to hang by their necks until they were dead.

However, after a long and bitter discussion, the court had included a recommendation for clemency for Mrs. Surratt. In the 1800s, society held women, especially mothers, in high esteem. Not only were they thought to be worthy of great respect, they were regarded as frail and dependent and in need of protection. As a result, anyone who hurt a woman was considered nothing less than a monster. The desire to protect women even extended to those who helped the enemy during the Civil War. Women caught red-handed as spies were not punished severely by either side. At the most, they were imprisoned for a short time. Male spies, however, were often shot.

All nine commission members thought that Mary Surratt was guilty, and six, the number needed for execution, had voted for the death penalty. Although the vote should have ended the discussion about Surratt's punishment, it failed to do so. The thought of a woman dangling at the end of a rope sickened some of the members, and they pleaded and argued with the six commission members who voted for the death penalty to change the punishment.

Each side argued its case with determination. Those who supported execution thought that simply imprisoning Surratt would encourage future conspirators to have women pull the trigger, knowing that they would be spared the worst punishment. These officials continued to demand the death penalty. Those who opposed execution insisted that Mary's age and sex should exempt her from the noose.

Eventually a compromise was reached. The panel would support the death penalty so that future conspirators, male and female, would think twice about assassinating anyone. It would also ask President Johnson to show mercy in this case by reducing Surratt's death sentence to life imprisonment. Five members supported this compromise; four did not.

The military court's decisions had to be signed by President Johnson, who had established the court, before the punishments could be carried out or made public. So after the panel had decided upon its plea for clemency on June 30, General Holt took the papers to the president. All eyes now turned to the White House.

5 FOUR HANGINGS

President Johnson was so ill when he received the commission's verdicts and recommended punishments on June 30 that he was unable to conduct any business, until July 5. Late that afternoon on July 5, he signed all of the commission's papers except the plea for clemency. Johnson ordered the military court to carry out the hangings between the hours of 10:00 A.M. and 2:00 P.M. on July 7. This rush to execute stunned the condemned, their lawyers, and the public, all of whom found out about the court's verdicts on July 6.

Even though there was little time to help Herold, Atzerodt, Paine, and Surratt, friends, relatives, and the prisoners' lawyers tried to do so anyway. Herold's sisters and Mrs. Surratt's daughter rushed to the White House to beg the president for mercy. Johnson was the only person who could change the penalties. He refused to do so.

Meanwhile, defense lawyers, who had also been turned down

Andrew Johnson was Lincoln's vice president.
Johnson, a Democrat, and Lincoln, a Republican, ran
on the Union ticket in 1864. Uniting the two parties
for this election was an attempt on the part of
political leaders to present a united front to the
South. To date, Johnson is the only president to have
been impeached. *Photo courtesy of the Library of
Congress.*

by the president, argued among themselves about how best to
help the condemned. After reviewing the cases once more, the
men singled out Mrs. Surratt, the only one they thought had any
possibility of being saved.

The lawyers examined every angle and finally decided that
their best chance was to try to obtain a writ of habeas corpus. This

writ not only can be used to force the courts to show a compelling reason to hold the accused, it can be used to challenge the right of a court to hold a particular trial. In this case, Surratt's lawyers planned to argue that trying Surratt in a military court had been unlawful. Therefore, the punishment should be set aside.

By the time this course of action was decided upon, it was early in the morning on July 7. Frederick Aiken and John Clampitt, who were now responsible for Mrs. Surratt's defense, pounded on the door of Judge Andrew B. Wylie, a member of the Supreme Court of the District of Columbia, at 2:00 A.M.. They persuaded Wylie to issue a writ. At 4:00 A.M., the writ was given to a U.S. marshal to deliver to the prison, which, if accepted, would stop Surratt's execution.

When President Johnson found out that a writ had been issued, he took quick action. No one, he argued, could use the writ of habeas corpus. It had been suspended during the war, and it had not been reinstated. He then demanded that this writ be ignored and that the executions take place that very day:

> I, Andrew Johnson, President of the United States, do
> hereby declare that the writ of Habeas Corpus has
> been heretofore suspended in such cases as this, and I
> do hereby especially suspend this writ, and direct that
> you proceed to execute the order heretofore given.[12]

Johnson gave his order to Attorney General Speed who took it to Judge Wylie. Wylie had no choice but to withdraw his writ.

When Herold, Atzerodt, Paine, and Surratt were told that they were to be hanged, they were given permission to have visitors. This included clergymen, who were sent for with great speed.

One of the ministers called by Paine was Reverend Abram Gillette, a pastor at Washington's First Baptist Church. Paine not only sought spiritual comfort from Gillette, he asked him to help Mrs. Surratt. Paine felt responsible for Surratt's predicament, believing that she would never have been arrested if he hadn't shown up at her home when the detectives were there. He said that he thought that he was doing the right thing when he attacked Seward, for he believed that he was acting as a Confederate soldier. Now he knew that what he did was wrong, and he had no will to live. But Mrs. Surratt, he insisted, did not deserve to die.

Paine also requested a visit with Captain Rath, an officer he knew. According to Rath, Paine said, "Captain, if I had two lives to give, I'd give one gladly to save Mrs. Surratt. I know that she is innocent. . . . She knew nothing about the conspiracy at all."[13]

Rath repeated Paine's statement to General Hartranft, who was in charge of the prison and the executions. Hartranft insisted that Paine's remarks be written down and forwarded to the president. Hartranft also wrote a letter to the president, which was hand delivered, saying that he thought that Paine was telling the truth. Johnson ignored both statements.

While defense lawyers struggled to find some other means to save Surratt, prison officials tried to make the condemned as comfortable as possible. They were moved into a large room on the first floor of the prison, given special meals, which all four refused, and three of the four were comforted by family members. Paine, however, had only told his lawyer about his real name on June 23, when he asked him to contact his father, Reverend George Powell, in Florida. As a result, the Powells were unaware that Lewis was in trouble. After being notified by letter, they did not have enough time to travel to Washington to see their son before he died.

Throughout the visiting period, the prisoners could hear carpenters sawing and pounding as they worked on the scaffold in the prison yard. Around 11:00, they heard the workers test the gallows, kicking out supports beneath the platforms, where the prisoners would soon stand. The crash of the falling timbers and the snap of the nooses, which now held 300-pound weights, unnerved even Paine, who up to now had accepted his fate with little show of emotion.

Believing that Mrs. Surratt would somehow be given a reprieve, Hartranft put off the executions as long as possible. But when no message had arrived by 1:00 P.M., Hartranft gave up hope, and he told his guards to bring the four prisoners to the yard. Soldiers, newspaper reporters, and witnesses, who were there only by invitation, turned toward the prison door as soon as it opened. One eyewitness said:

Suddenly the [door] opens, the troops spring to their feet and stand to order; the flags go up. . . . First came a woman—a middle aged woman dressed in black, bonneted and veiled, walking between two bareheaded priests. . . . Four soldiers with muskets at shoulder followed, and a captain led the way to the gallows. The second party escorted a small shambling man [Atzerodt] . . . preceded by two officers, flanked by a Lutheran clergyman, and followed, as by his predecessor, by an armed squad. . . . The third, preacher and party, clustered about a shabby boy whose limbs tottered as he progressed [Herold].[14]

The last person to enter the yard was Lewis Paine. He was escorted by two officers and two ministers, including Reverend Gillette.

All of the members of the party, prisoners, soldiers, and clergymen, climbed the stairs to the platform, where they were seated and shielded from the hot sun by umbrellas. After General Hartranft read the findings of the panel, prayers on behalf of the prisoners were given by the ministers and priests. When the last "amen" was said, the condemned were ordered to rise. Their arms and legs were bound and hoods were placed over their heads. Mrs. Surratt was so weak at this point that she had to be supported in order to remain standing. As soon as the last knot was tied, a noose was placed and secured around each neck.

There was a pause now, as Hartranft looked back at the yard's door one last time. He had assigned one of his best couriers to the White House, where he stood ready to bring a last-minute

Before Mary Surratt, Lewis Paine, David Herold, and George Atzerodt were hanged, they were seated on the execution platform. The charges against them were read, and then a brief prayer was said. The umbrellas were used to shield the prisoners from the hot sun. *Below:* When the trapdoor on the platform was dropped, all four shoeless prisoners fell to their deaths at the same time. *Photos courtesy of the Library of Congress.*

message should the president change his mind. No one, however, had entered the yard.

As the witnesses and executioners waited for the dreaded moment, silence descended on the crowd. Suddenly, two loud claps were heard, Hartranft's signal to knock away the supports beneath the condemned. At 1:26 P.M., the four prisoners dropped together, twisting and turning for almost half an hour. They were then cut down, placed in wooden coffins, and buried next to the gallows.

Once the prisoners were pronounced dead, commission members, Stanton, and Johnson sighed with relief. They believed that the worst was behind them. They couldn't have been more mistaken.

6 ANOTHER TRIAL?

Shortly after Mary Surratt and the others were buried, War Department officials set out with great determination to finish the assassination case. They still had to select a prison site for the four convicted prisoners, try Jefferson Davis, and find John Surratt. And then there was the question of what to do with the rest of the Confederate officials listed in President Johnson's May 2 proclamation, most of whom remained at large.

The convicted prisoners were dealt with first. The War Department held Mudd, Spangler, Arnold, and O'Laughlin in the penitentiary where they had been tried while officials looked for the most secure prison possible. The convicts were given some privileges, including exercising in the prison yard, where they walked past four new graves every day. On July 17, guards moved the men to Dry Tortugas, a remote, sandy island about eighty miles southwest of the tip of Florida. This island was almost entirely covered by Fort Jefferson, which housed many soldiers as well as military prisoners.

Once the prisoners were safely stowed away for the rest of their lives, department officials reexamined the government's case against Jefferson Davis. Although Davis had been arrested for participating in the Lincoln murder plot, some department members thought that he should be tried for treason instead. After all, he had led the seceded states. Others insisted that the department pursue the original charge.

Since none of the Confederate soldiers or their officers had been charged with treason, War Department officials were leery about trying a Confederate leader as a traitor. Furthermore, according to the U.S. Constitution, anyone accused of treason has to be tried in a civil court in the state where the crime was said to have occurred. In this case, Davis would be tried in Virginia. No one believed for a moment that a jury of Virginians would find Davis guilty of anything, for even though the South had lost the war, he was a hero to them. So, for a while, the idea of trying Davis as a traitor was set aside.

On the other hand, trying Davis for the assassination of Lincoln presented some very serious problems now, even though the department was convinced of his guilt. The execution of Mary Surratt had appalled many Americans, who, until July 7, had been screaming for justice and a little blood. Now they lashed out at Stanton, Holt, and Johnson and called them murderers. The department feared that if Davis was convicted and executed, his hanging would add greatly to this outrage, especially in the South.

In addition, just holding a trial was risky for the department, since some evidence used at the first hearing was now being challenged. A more public examination of this so-called proof might bring into question the fairness of the first trial, which would enrage all Americans.

So department officials would have preferred to have had lots of time to deal with the Davis case, hoping eventually to discover some easy solution to the dilemma he presented. This wasn't possible, though, for two reasons. First, Jefferson Davis's health, which was not strong to begin with, was failing rapidly. This was due in large part to the fact that he lived in a cold, damp cell in Fort Monroe. When Varina Davis learned about her husband's living conditions, she feared for his life, and she immediately began to push for his release. Eventually Varina gained the support of a number of Americans who demanded— loudly!—that the government try Davis or free him.

The War Department was also being pressured by the House of Representatives to hold a trial. When the House met in December 1865, the first time since Lincoln's assassination, Southern legislators, who had been elected by their states to represent them in Washington, were standing at the door waiting for admission. Some Northern representatives were loath to accept Southerners for a number of reasons, including the suspicion that Davis and other Confederates had been part of the Lincoln murder plot. These representatives then asked President Johnson for a report on the Davis case to help them decide if any—or all—of the new representatives should be denied entry.

Meanwhile, wanting more time to figure out what to do with

the former Confederate president, Secretary Stanton asked Johnson to refuse to give the House anything, a request that Johnson honored. This angered the House, which was now led by a group of men known as Radical Republicans, some of whom were eager to punish former Confederate leaders. These Republicans suspected that Johnson was protecting Davis and that no trial would ever be held. Old rumors about Johnson, who was a Southerner by birth, suddenly reappeared and spread like wildfire in Congress. Some said that he had been a spy for Jefferson Davis during the war. Others repeated stories about Johnson being in league with Booth. Hadn't Johnson profited by Lincoln's death? they asked.

Not content to sit by while Johnson stalled, on April 9, 1866, the House of Representatives instructed its Judiciary Committee to investigate the charges against Davis. If the committee could find enough evidence to try the former Confederate president for murder, the House actually planned to pass a law that would bring Davis to trial. Johnson challenged the representatives' right to do this, and he seethed with anger at the repetition of old, and in his opinion, scandalous, stories.

Later that month, General Holt appeared before the Judiciary Committee to present his case against Davis. Holt believed more strongly than ever that Davis was behind Lincoln's death, and he said so, repeating the evidence used at the trial. Holt relied heavily on Sanford Conover, who had once been in Davis's War Department and had said that he had been present when John Surratt had delivered messages from Davis approving the plot. Conover not only stuck to his story, he said that he could produce eight new witnesses who had given written statements to him that would link Davis to Booth. Holt suggested that the committee interview them, and it quickly agreed to do so.

At first, Holt's assistant, Colonel L.C. Turner, could find only one of the newest witnesses, William Campbell. He turned out to be the opposite of what Conover had promised. After only a few questions, Campbell broke down. His original statement, he said, was a lie. "This is all false: I must make a clean breast of it; I can't stand it any longer."[15] Campbell, whose real name was Joseph A. Hoare, explained that Sanford Conover had told him what to say.

Eventually, the other seven witnesses were found, and they all told the same story. Conover, who had lied at the trial, had talked them into giving false statements. Davis had at one time ordered the arrest and imprisonment of Conover while he was in Richmond. Conover was trying to get even, and the eight witnesses, who had no love for Davis, had agreed to help him. Conover was eventually arrested, tried for perjury, and sentenced to ten years in prison.

Although Holt tried to link Davis and Booth through other witnesses, upon cross-examination they turned out to be no better than Conover. Holt refused to give up, however, seeking out new witnesses. The department had to prove that Davis had committed an act of war in order to try him in a military court.

While Holt struggled, unsuccessfully, to save his case, the U.S. Supreme Court announced a landmark decision in late 1866 that greatly affected the department. In 1864, Lambdin P. Milligan was arrested in Indiana and tried in a military court for a long list of offenses that included spying for the South and trying to free Confederate prisoners held in the North. He was sentenced to death by hanging. While Milligan languished in prison, his lawyers appealed his case all the way to the Supreme Court, arguing that their client, a civilian, should not have been tried by a military commission.

The Supreme Court agreed. Justice David Davis, who spoke for the majority, said that there were many reasons why a military trial for Milligan was inappropriate. One of these reasons was the fact that every American has the right, when arrested, to be tried in a court established by law. Military courts are established by the president. Also, the Court said, every American has the right to be judged by a jury of his or her peers. Suspects tried in military courts are judged by military officers, who are hardly an average American's equal. And finally, since civil courts were open, there was no need to turn to another court. Even if a civil court wasn't meeting at the time, Justice Davis added, the suspect could be held until it did. What was the hurry? the Court wondered. When Milligan's lawyer had asked to have the trial moved to a civil court, the justices concluded, the request should have been honored.

The Milligan decision stunned the War Department. This decision meant that Jefferson Davis—as well as all the other Confederates wanted in the Lincoln murder plot—could not be tried in a military court. After reading and rereading the Court's decision, the department reluctantly turned Davis over to a civil court in Virginia.

This court found a clever way to solve the problem that Davis presented. When he was brought into the courtroom on May 13, 1867, two years after he had been arrested, the prosecution announced that it was not ready to present any case against Davis. The court then granted bail to Davis and set him free. The court's decision brought great joy to Davis's family and his supporters, and it limited criticism from those who regarded him as a criminal, since holding a trial was still possible.

The Milligan decision affected more people than Milligan and Davis, though. It also meant that all of the trials of civilians held in military courts during and after the war, including the trial of the eight prisoners accused of being members of the Lincoln murder plot, were illegal. This news brought dismay to the families of the four prisoners who had been executed and hope to the families of the men imprisoned on Dry Tortugas.

While the War Department was reeling from the Supreme Court decision, the department received more bad news: John Surratt had been arrested. Surratt had been on an assignment for the Confederacy when he had heard about Lincoln's assassination. After delivering messages to Montreal from Richmond, he had been sent to Elmira, New York, where a large number of Southern prisoners of war were being held. His assignment was to study the possibility of arranging a breakout for the soldiers.

When Surratt had learned that Booth was Lincoln's assassin, John had correctly feared arrest, and he had sought safety outside the United States. Before the war began, Surratt had planned to be a priest, visiting a number of monasteries over the years, where he had met many clergymen. After the assassination, he had convinced several of them that his life was in dan-

John Surratt is pictured here in his official papal guard uniform. Surratt was set free after his trial. He tried to make a living by giving speeches about the kidnapping plot and his involvement with Booth. However, many people were appalled by the fact that Surratt did nothing to help his mother when she was imprisoned, and they refused to attend his lectures. As a result, his speaking career was very short. *Photo courtesy of the Library of Congress.*

ger, and they had helped him reach England. From there he had traveled to Italy, where he had become a guard at the Vatican, the Pope's residence. Surratt had remained in Italy until officials had tried to arrest him. After escaping to Egypt, he was finally taken into custody on November 27, 1866. Surratt arrived in the United States in February 1867. Since military trials for civilians had been ruled out by this time, John Surratt was tried for the murder of Lincoln in a civil court in the District of Columbia. Surratt's trial began on June 10, 1867.

The defense, led by John O. Carlisle, dominated the courtroom. Carlisle presented a letter written by Booth as well as his diary, to prove that a kidnapping plot had really existed. This, the prosecutors argued, was what Surratt had been involved in, not murder.

BOOTH'S LETTER

John Wilkes Booth left a letter with his sister for safekeeping sometime in late 1864. The letter is very formal, and most historians believe that he wrote it with publication in mind. It was produced at John Surratt's trial to prove that a kidnapping plot really existed. Booth said, in part:

To whom it may concern:

Right or wrong, God judge me, not man. For be my motive good or bad, of one thing I am sure, the lasting condemnation of the North. . . . For four years I have waited, hoped and prayed for the dark clouds to break and for a restoration of our former sunshine. To wait longer would be a crime. All hope for peace is dead. My prayers have proved as idle as my hopes. . . .

I have ever held the South were right. . . . But Lincoln's policy is only preparing a way for [its] total annihilation. . . . The South can make no choice. It is either extermination or slavery for themselves (worse than death) to draw from. I know my choice. . . .

My love is for the South alone. Nor do I deem it a dishonor in attempting to make for her a prisoner of this man to whom she owes so much of [her] misery. . . .

A Confederate doing duty upon his own responsibility.

J. Wilkes Booth[16]

Next, the defense destroyed the credibility of the prosecution's two main witnesses, John Lloyd and Louis Weichmann, both of whom had been so instrumental in persuading the commission that Mary Surratt was guilty. The defense did this by analyzing and challenging almost everything that the men had said at the first trial.

Lloyd was not eager to testify, and he gave short and evasive answers. Under cross-examination, however, John Surratt's lawyer was able to get Lloyd to admit that he had a drinking problem. The defense also forced him to admit that he had been drunk when Mary Surratt had been at the tavern on the day of Lincoln's assassination. After a few more questions, Lloyd confessed that he really hadn't remembered what she had said or done that day. Instead, he had simply supported whatever anyone else had said had happened.

Lloyd, who had been imprisoned as a possible conspirator shortly after Lincoln had died, was then questioned about promises made by a detective named Cottingham who had interviewed him. Lloyd said that after he had agreed to testify against Mary Surratt, he had been told by Cottingham that "the government would protect me and my property and support me, and see that I was returned home."[17] There was no small stir in the courtroom when this information was given.

Weichmann's credibility was attacked next. It had been under fire since July 11, 1865, when a startling statement by John P. Brophy had appeared in the Washington *Constitutional Union*. This statement had been sent to President Johnson on July 7, the day of the executions. When Johnson had ignored it, Brophy had turned to the paper to make his information public. Brophy, a friend of Weichmann's, had insisted that Weichmann had lied on the stand to save his own life. Brophy's statement was introduced at Surratt's trial. He said, in part:

> He [Weichmann] told me that he was arrested as a conspirator and threatened with death by Mr. Stanton and Mr. Burnett [one of the prosecutors at the trial] unless he would at once reveal all about the assassination—they alleging that he knew all about it.
>
> He told me he would rather be hooted at as a spy and informer, and do anything rather than be tried as a conspirator, and have his future hopes blasted.
>
> He told me since the close of the trial that once while some of these men were in the house with John, Mrs. Surratt called John aside and said to him, "John! there is something going on. I am afraid. . . . Why do these men come here?". . . Weichmann also told me John did not tell her why the men were there or what they were about.
>
> Since the trial closed, he told me he thought Mrs. Surratt to be innocent.[18]

Lewis Carland, another friend of Weichmann's, testified that Weichmann had made similar statements to him. Together, Brophy's and Carland's testimony so damaged Weichmann's reputation that little of what he said afterward at this trial was believed. The fact that he had been given a secure position in the government cast even more doubt upon his reliability as an impartial witness.

The defense summed up its case in early August. The jury could not make a decision regarding Surratt's guilt; four members voted for conviction, eight did not. Surratt was set free on bail. He was never again brought into court.

John Surratt's lawyer not only successfully defended his client and proved that some of the evidence given at the first trial was far from the truth, he made public for the first time the military commission's recommendation that Mary Surratt's life be spared. Americans thought that the fact that she had been tried illegally and that falsified evidence had been given against her was bad enough, but to learn that her life could have been saved was more than most men and women could handle gracefully. The public reacted with outbursts of anger, disgust, and outright contempt for Johnson, Stanton, and the military commission.

These men struggled to defend themselves. Johnson insisted that he had never seen the plea for clemency, that it had been withheld from him by Holt under the orders of Stanton. Holt insisted that he had delivered the plea, and Stanton denied ordering Holt to withhold anything. None of them was able to prove his argument and each fought off accusations until he died.

The controversy that followed only made a bad situation worse. By this time, President Johnson and Congress were embroiled in a bitter debate about how to treat the South and who was going to direct a Reconstruction program, the president or

Congress. The Radical Republicans were so determined to have their way that they pushed through the Tenure of Office Act. This act made it illegal for the president to fire anyone holding office who had been approved by the Senate. Congress did this to prevent Johnson from replacing officials who supported Congress with men who would back him. This included cabinet officials, such as Secretary Stanton.

The conflict between Johnson and Stanton came to a head on August 12, only days after the plea for clemency for Mary Surratt was made public. Johnson had long believed, correctly, that Stanton was one of the Radical Republicans and that he was trying to undermine Johnson's Reconstruction program. Johnson was also convinced that Stanton had told Holt to withhold Surratt's plea to embarrass him. Worse yet, Johnson had received a letter from the now notorious Sanford Conover indicating that several senators, with the backing of General Holt, had asked Conover to make up some evidence that would link Johnson to Lincoln's assassination. The president was dead certain that Stanton was behind this, so Johnson fired his secretary of war.

While Stanton barricaded himself in his office, refusing to admit that Johnson had any power to fire him, an outraged Congress began to put together a case to impeach the president and remove him from office. The House of Representatives began the process by making a long list of grievances, which included violating the Tenure of Office Act. Hearings began in the House in February 1868.

The House's charges and evidence were turned over to the

Senate on March 25. If it found the president guilty as charged, it could remove him from office. On May 26, 1868, the senators cast their ballots. Johnson was found not guilty by one vote.

Although Johnson remained in office, his power was severely limited. However, this did not prevent him from trying to make up for some miscarriages of justice. On February 8, 1869, convinced that Booth, Paine, Atzerodt, and Herold were the only people involved in the Lincoln murder plot, Johnson pardoned Dr. Mudd, Samuel Arnold, and Edward Spangler. It was too late to pardon Michael O'Laughlin. He had died some months before on Dry Tortugas during an outbreak of yellow fever. The prisoners were released from Fort Jefferson shortly after, and they returned to their homes to lead quiet, uneventful lives.

In March, Johnson ordered the bodies of Booth, Mrs. Surratt, Paine, Herold, and Atzerodt to be exhumed and sent to their families. This was an act of kindness on the part of Johnson, who hoped that a final burial would be a way to help these families end their ordeal.

These acts should also have ended the chapter on the Lincoln murder conspiracy, but they did not do so. Americans no longer trusted Johnson, Stanton, and the military commission. Believing that all three had lied and refusing to give up on a grand conspiracy theory, the public began its own investigation—an investigation that had some strange results over the years.

7 AFTERMATH

Many Americans simply would not believe that John Wilkes Booth could carry out a plot to kill the president without help. So they cast about for suspects, extraordinary suspects, for surely no ordinary person could destroy a man of Lincoln's standing. In the process, they created myths that last to this very day.

Some rumormongers thought that Pope Pius IX, the leader of the Roman Catholic Church, was behind Lincoln's death. Throughout the Civil War, immigrants from European countries poured into the North to seek work on farms and in industries that were thriving due to government orders for supplies for the army. Many of the new immigrants were Irish, who brought with them their Catholic faith. Their religious beliefs set them apart from their predominately Protestant neighbors, who often treated the newcomers with great suspicion. This was due, in large part, to the fact that many Americans thought that Catholics were more loyal to the Pope than they were to their country. This suspicion grew throughout the war, especially when many Irish immigrants refused to volunteer to serve in the Union Army.

As a result, when the Confederate conspiracy fell apart and the South could not be blamed for Lincoln's death, the Catholic Church became a convenient scapegoat for many Americans. When the first trial began and newspaper reporters mistakenly announced that all of the suspects about to be tried for the assassination were Catholic, more than a few Americans were willing to put the blame on the Church then and there. Others joined this group when Catholic priests protested loudly against Mary Surratt's execution. More joined when John Surratt was arrested and the public learned that not only had priests harbored Surratt when authorities first tried to arrest him, he was working for the Pope himself! What more proof, anti-Catholics shouted, did anyone need? These people could never determine what the Pope's motive might have been, nor could they provide one shred of evidence that linked him to any plot to kill Lincoln. Even so, this rumor persisted well into the 1900s.

Conspiracy believers who did not accept the idea that the Pope had plotted Lincoln's murder used circumstantial evidence to accuse a lot of people in the capital of the assassination. The list of suspects included the president, senators, and cabinet members. Eventually, a number of people claimed to have found the truth.

One of these people was Otto Eisenschiml, a history buff. He had long been bothered by a number of questions about Lincoln's assassination. Why did General Grant change his mind at the last minute and not attend the play with Lincoln at Ford's Theatre? Why wasn't Lincoln given more protection? Immediately after the assassination, guards at the city's exits were supposed to receive telegrams warning them that an assassin might try to leave the city. However, Sergeant Cobb at the Navy Yard bridge had not received this message. Why not? Booth's diary was missing pages. What had these pages contained and who had removed them? Booth was shot against orders. Why did this happen? And why were some members of the government attacked—or targeted for attack—but not others?

After years of research, Otto Eisenschiml believed that he had found the answers to his questions, and, at long last, the man he believed to be the real leader of the conspiracy, Secretary of War Stanton. Eisenschiml became suspicious of Stanton when he learned that the secretary had ordered Grant not to attend the play. Eisenschiml realized that this made Lincoln's position less secure because it meant that Lincoln would not have the protection that Grant, and the staff that always accompanied him, could provide.

Eisenschiml's suspicion of Stanton grew when the author learned that it was Stanton who controlled the messages sent to guards about watching for an assassin. Out of all of the guards watching all of the exits from Washington, the only soldier who had not been warned watched the very exit that Booth had planned to take. Eisenschiml believed that this couldn't have been a mere coincidence.

In addition, Eisenschiml had learned that the person who had the best access to Booth's diary, and therefore could have removed pages at will, was Stanton. It had been turned over to him as soon as it was brought to Washington. Eisenschiml didn't know what was on the missing pages, but he could guess—something that incriminated the secretary. Not only did Stanton have to remove the pages, Eisenschiml added, he had to make sure that Booth didn't talk to investigators. Therefore, Booth was shot because Stanton ordered at least one man to do so.

Stanton, who obviously wouldn't order an attack on himself, had one or even two motives for attacking the others. Stanton may have believed that if the country was kept in turmoil, he would continue to hold extraordinary power, as he had done throughout the war. Or Stanton may have thought that by removing Lincoln, Seward, and Johnson, the Radical Republicans could dominate the government and design a Reconstruction program to their liking.

Eisenschiml was only partially correct in his statements. Stanton really had ordered Grant to stay away from the theatre that night. The secretary had heard many rumors about angry Confederates wanting to avenge the South's loss by killing Union leaders. As a result, he did everything he could to persuade government officials to stay home. To try to change the president's plans, Stanton ordered Grant not to go as well as at least one other general whom Lincoln had invited.

Because Stanton wouldn't provide more than the usual soldier escort in order to make Lincoln change his mind, Lincoln turned to the local police who assigned John Parker to guard the president's box. Why Parker left his post is not certain, but he was not under orders from Stanton to do so. Stanton was not

Parker's boss. Some historians believe that the president told Parker to find a spot where he could enjoy the play, as Lincoln had often done in the past. Whatever his reason was, it was acceptable to his superiors. Parker was never punished.

Sergeant Cobb at the Navy Yard bridge did not immediately receive a telegram warning him to be on the lookout for at least one murderer until it was too late. This was due to the fact that the military telegraph system did not have a station near the bridge. It was the only exit that was not close to the telegraph line, so messages had to be delivered to this post by a courier. Cobb was warned, but when he received the shocking news, Booth had managed to escape.

Booth's diary was missing eighteen pages, just as Eisenschiml said. However, Stanton did not remove them. Soldiers testified at John Surratt's trial that these pages were missing when they took the diary from Booth as he lay dying on Garrett's porch. Also, friends mentioned that Booth had the habit of tearing blank pages from his diary to make notes.

Stanton was not targeted by Booth for several very good reasons. Booth had a limited number of accomplices, and not all of them were willing to commit murder. The decision to kill was made quickly, even though Booth had long grumbled about doing so when Lincoln was too valuable as a potential kidnap victim to murder. Therefore, Booth, who did not have enough time to find more accomplices on such short notice, could not have ordered the death of all federal leaders on April 14, no matter how much he wished to do so. Instead, Booth had to decide how best to use his fellow conspirators. Since Stanton was known to be well guarded—he feared assassination even if Lincoln didn't—a skilled killer would have had great difficulty murdering him. Booth's accomplices were not skilled assassins, something Booth must have realized.

And finally, Booth was shot, not to keep him from talking, but to keep him from shooting others. A number of soldiers at the scene testified to this.

Even though there was no proof to support Eisenschiml's accusations, he gained a large audience when he published his conclusions in 1937 in a book titled *Why Was Lincoln Murdered?* Interest in Lincoln's assassination, more than seventy years after it had taken place, was still so high that Eisenschiml's book became a best-seller. In fact, his book made such an impact that, over the following years, other investigators actually looked for proof to support the author's charges.

In 1961 Ray Neff claimed that he had found a letter hidden inside an old book that he purchased in a bookstore that specialized in rare texts. The letter, according to Neff, was written by Lafayette C. Baker, who had been in charge of detectives in the War Department during the assassination investigation and one of the men who had buried Booth. The letter claimed that Stanton was behind the plot. He had been assisted by "eleven members of Congress . . . no less than twelve Army officers, three Naval officers, and at least 24 civilians, of which one was a governor of a loyal state."[19] This was heady stuff for anyone who believed in a conspiracy. Eventually, though, the letter was exposed as a fraud.

In 1971, more information about the Lincoln conspiracy was

supposedly found. Two authors, David Balsiger and Charles E. Sellier, Jr., wrote a book titled *The Lincoln Conspiracy*, which was published in 1977. These authors claimed that there was new proof that Stanton was guilty—the missing pages from Booth's diary. These pages had been found among the papers of one of Stanton's descendants. This unidentified relative would not let the writers see the pages. Instead, he or she wrote a summary of them for the authors. Even though these entries, as well as several newly discovered diaries, were never proved to have been the real thing, *The Lincoln Conspiracy* not only sold well, it became the basis for a movie about the assassination. This only further spread the accusations against Stanton.

Conspiracy theories were helped along by at least twenty men who, at some time in the years following Lincoln's death, claimed to be John Wilkes Booth. Each man insisted, sometimes on his deathbed, that someone other than Booth had been killed. Some of the would-be Booths said that they had gotten away with the help of Stanton. Why these men wanted to be Booth was never made clear.

After all of the make-believe Booths passed away, the legend that Booth had escaped and was not buried in the family plot was kept alive by showmen who claimed that they had Booth's skull. For the price of a ticket, people attending certain carnivals or traveling shows could see Booth's head. At one time, at least four different skulls—all supposedly belonging to Booth—were on display in various parts of the country.

While men were claiming to be Booth, a final conspiracy involving Lincoln was in the works. Booth had once wanted to ransom Lincoln for 35,000 Confederate soldiers. In 1876, eleven years after Lincoln had been buried in Springfield, Illinois, Big Jim Kneally, the leader of a counterfeit gang in Illinois, wanted to ransom Lincoln's corpse for one man, a forger named Ben Boyd. Boyd was imprisoned in Joliet, Illinois. Big Jim had tried to find another counterfeiter to take Boyd's place, but no one could match Boyd's skills in the phony-money business. So Big Jim had to get him out of prison and back at work.

Kneally lost little time in selecting men to carry out his wild scheme. This group included a professional body snatcher from Chicago, Lewis Swegles, who bragged that he was the best of the lot in all of Chicago. He claimed that he had routinely supplied medical schools with most of their cadavers for years and had established a record that no one could rival.

Kneally's men were given specific tasks. On the night of November 7, 1876, when all eyes would be on the presidential election, two men would break into the tomb. Swegles would steal the body, after making sure that it was Lincoln's. Two other men would take the corpse to a designated spot in the sand dunes along Lake Michigan, where they would hide the coffin. Once the body was buried beneath drifting sand, another member of the gang would begin negotiations with the government.

The plot was doomed from the beginning. Informants had warned local officials about the potential theft, and the so-called master body snatcher was an undercover agent. Most of the plotters were arrested as soon as the digging started at Lincoln's tomb; the rest were picked up shortly after.

At first, the story seemed so far-fetched that few believed that

In 1901, Lincoln's body, in the large wooden box, and the bodies of his wife and three of their sons were moved from separate burial sites in Springfield to be housed in one location. The new tomb was more secure and made stealing Lincoln's body nearly impossible. *Photo courtesy of the Illinois State Historical Library.*

such a thing could actually happen. In fact, many of the nation's best-known newspapers refused to run the story for several days. Once the story was verified, however, it didn't take Americans long to react. Many thought that Big Jim would never have tried to try to pull off such a crime all by himself. He had to have a mastermind or two behind him, they said. The most logical culprits? Former Confederates, of course.

While Southerners shook their heads in bewilderment, officials in Springfield began to take steps that would make stealing

Lincoln's body impossible in the future. His coffin was secretly moved several times until 1901, when a new monument in the cemetery was ready and a secure burial method was devised. After positive identification of the corpse was made, Lincoln's body was buried and then covered with tons of concrete.

Although Lincoln is now at rest, the grand conspiracy theory is not. History buffs continue to probe the president's assassination, and some have even asked Congress to investigate Lincoln's death. They also continue to ask the main question that has long surrounded the conspiracy, ignoring the proof that has been provided to date: Were all of the conspirators identified? And finally, these history buffs, like many Americans, join in the debate about the aftermath of the assassination, wondering aloud if justice was served.

NOTES

1. Dorothy Meserve Kunhardt and Philip B. Kunhardt, Jr., *Twenty Days* (New York: Harper & Row, 1965), p. 11.

2. Katharine Jones, *Ladies of Richmond* (Indianapolis: Bobbs-Merrill Company, Inc., 1962), pp. 281, 282.

3. Samuel Carter, *The Riddle of Dr. Mudd* (New York: Putnam, 1974), p. 71.

4. Philip B. Kunhardt, Jr., Philip B. Kunhardt III, and Peter W. Kunhardt, *Lincoln: An Illustrated Biography* (New York: Alfred A. Knopf, 1992), p. 362.

5. Elden C. Weckesser, *His Name Was Mudd: The Life of Dr. Samuel A. Mudd, Who Treated the Fleeing John Wilkes Booth* (Jefferson, North Carolina: McFarland & Company, 1991), p. 219.

6. Kunhardt, Kunhardt, and Kunhardt, *Lincoln: An Illustrated Biography*, p. 366.

7. Weckesser, *His Name Was Mudd*, pp. 214, 215.

8. William Hanchett, *The Lincoln Murder Conspiracies* (Urbana: University of Illinois Press, 1986), p. 64.

9. Hanchett, *The Lincoln Murder Conspiracies*, p. 72.

10. Betty J. Ownsbey, *Alias "Paine": Lewis Thornton Powell, the Mystery Man of the Lincoln Conspiracy* (Jefferson, North Carolina: McFarland & Company, 1993), p. 82.

11. Louis J. Weichmann, *A True History of the Assassination of Abraham Lincoln and of the Conspiracy of 1865* (New York: Alfred A. Knopf, 1975), p. 252.

12. Guy W. Moore, *The Case of Mrs. Surratt: Her Controversial Trial and Execution for Conspiracy in the Lincoln Assassination* (Norman: University of Oklahoma Press, 1954), p. 58.

13. Ownsbey, *Alias "Paine"*, p. 139.

14. Ownsbey, *Alias "Paine"*, p. 144.

15. Hanchett, *The Lincoln Murder Conspiracies*, p. 79.

16. Carter, *The Riddle of Dr. Mudd*, p. 79.

17. Moore, *The Case of Mrs. Surratt*, p. 79.

18. Moore, *The Case of Mrs. Surratt*, pp. 63, 64.

19. Hanchett, *The Lincoln Murder Conspiracies*, p. 216.

BIBLIOGRAPHY

Bishop, Jim. *The Day Lincoln Was Shot*. New York: Bantam Books, 1955.

Carter, Samuel. *The Riddle of Dr. Mudd*. New York: Putnam, 1974.

Davis, William C. *Jefferson Davis: The Man and His Hour*. New York: HarperCollins Publishers, 1991.

Hanchett, William. *The Lincoln Murder Conspiracies*. Urbana: University of Illinois Press, 1986.

Jones, Katharine. *Ladies of Richmond*. Indianapolis: Bobbs-Merrill Company, Inc., 1962.

Kunhardt, Dorothy Meserve, and Philip B. Kunhardt, Jr. *Twenty Days*. New York: Harper & Row, 1965.

Kunhardt, Philip B., Jr., Philip B. Kunhardt III, and Peter W. Kunhardt. *Lincoln: An Illustrated Biography*. New York: Alfred A. Knopf, 1992.

Lewis, Lloyd. *The Assassination of Lincoln: History and Myth.* Lincoln: University of Nebraska Press, 1994 (c. 1929).

McKitrick, Eric L. *Andrew Johnson and Reconstruction.* Chicago: University of Chicago Press, 1960.

Moore, Guy W. *The Case of Mrs. Surratt: Her Controversial Trial and Execution for Conspiracy in the Lincoln Assassination.* Norman: University of Oklahoma Press, 1954.

Ownsbey, Betty J. *Alias "Paine": Lewis Thornton Powell, the Mystery Man of the Lincoln Conspiracy.* Jefferson, North Carolina: McFarland & Company, 1993.

Weckesser, Elden C. *His Name Was Mudd: The Life of Dr. Samuel A. Mudd, Who Treated the Fleeing John Wilkes Booth.* Jefferson, North Carolina: McFarland & Company, 1991.

Weichmann, Louis J. *A True History of the Assassination of Abraham Lincoln and of the Conspiracy of 1865.* New York: Alfred A. Knopf, 1975.

FOR MORE INFORMATION

To learn more about the people and events mentioned in this book, check out the following:

Lincoln: A Photobiography by Russell Freedman (New York: Clarion, 1987). This award-winning book discusses Lincoln's life, and it is richly illustrated with photographs, a number of which were little known until this text was published.

The Assassination of Abraham Lincoln by Robert Jakoubek (Brookfield, CT: Millbrook Press, 1993). Jakoubek's short book discusses the events leading up to the assassination before explaining in detail what happened in Ford's Theatre on the night of April 14.

Dr. Samuel A. Mudd and the Lincoln Assassination by John E. McHale (Englewood Cliffs, NJ: Dillon Silver Burdett, 1995). McHale's text examines Mudd's role in the controversy and details Mudd's life before and after Lincoln's death.

Andrew Johnson: Rebuilding the Union by Cathy East Dubowski (Englewood Cliffs, NJ: Silver Burdett Press, 1991). Dubowski's book is part of Silver Burdett's series on the Civil War. It discusses Johnson's political career, the problems that he faced in trying to reunite the country, and his bitter struggle with the Radical Republicans, including Edwin Stanton.

Jefferson Davis by Perry Scott King (Philadelphia: Chelsea House Publishers, 1990). King's book examines Davis's life, his role in American politics before the war, which was significant, and his leadership of the Confederacy.

INDEX

Page numbers are given in bold for individual portraits.